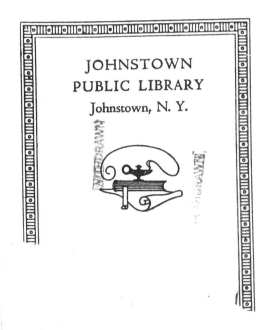

AMERICAN HISTORICAL SOURCES SERIES:
Research and Interpretation

LORMAN RATNER, Editor

PRENTICE-HALL INTERNATIONAL, INC., *London*
PRENTICE-HALL OF AUSTRALIA PTY. LTD., *Sydney*
PRENTICE-HALL OF CANADA LTD., *Toronto*
PRENTICE-HALL OF INDIA PRIVATE LTD., *New Delhi*
PRENTICE-HALL OF JAPAN, INC., *Tokyo*

ANTIMASONRY

Lorman Ratner
Herbert H. Lehman College
The City University of New York

ANTIMASONRY

The Crusade
and the Party

Prentice-Hall, Inc., Englewood Cliffs, New Jersey

To David Brion Davis

Current printing (last digit):
10 9 8 7 6 5 4 3 2 1

© 1969 by PRENTICE-HALL, INC.
Englewood Cliffs, New Jersey

Library of Congress Catalog Card No.: 72–88712

Printed in the United States of America
13–038513–1

EDITOR'S FOREWORD

Antimasonry: The Crusade and the Party is a volume in the American Historical Sources Series, a series devoted to the exploration of aspects of American history and to the process of interpreting historical evidence. The introduction to each volume will be followed by some of the original documents used to prepare the essay. In this way readers are invited to share in the experience of turning raw evidence into history.

When I considered topics that would be appropriate for this series, Antimasonry seemed to qualify on several counts. First, it offered the opportunity to study the Jacksonian era from a different perspective; although his name has been given to the age, Andrew Jackson and his supporters were only part of a much larger group of actors. Second, a study of Antimasonry involved dealing with both the politics and the temper of a time; Antimasonry was a crusade in an age of crusades. Third, Antimasonry was not limited to just one period of time. The existence of Antimasonic feeling in the eighteenth century made possible some comparisons of both Antimasonic sentiments, the content of which changed over time, and the societies in which Antimasonry provoked interest. Finally, when we study Antimasonry, questions arise such as what motivated men to join the Antimasonic crusade and become active in the Party, and what problems resulted when a crusade and a party combined. I have not attempted to answer these questions, but rather, to point out problems, suggest some lines to follow, and provide some material for study, all of which will be of use to students for pursuing the subject on their own.

LORMAN RATNER

Herbert H. Lehman College
The City University of New York

CONTENTS

vii

Antimasonry: The Crusade
and the Party

On the 11th of September in 1826 three men kidnapped a prisoner from the jail in Batavia, New York. The victim was William Morgan, a Mason who was planning to publish the secret rituals of that Fraternity. The reactions to this isolated event in that small village in western New York ranged from public demands to punish the kidnappers, to widespread denunciation of the Masons, to a state legislative investigation and, finally, to the formation of political parties on both the state and the national levels.

In searching for an explanation for this overreaction to such a relatively insignificant incident, we must ask such questions as what was there about the Masonic Fraternity that caused so many people to view it with suspicion? Were there reasons, other than the Morgan incident, that caused Americans of that time to single out Masonry as an evil to be eliminated? And since many Americans of the period certainly failed to respond to Antimasonry, what characterized an Antimason? But the historian of the Antimasonic crusade must recognize that what motivated men to attack the Fraternity, what caused them to see in it such a danger, and what led them to such extremes of rhetoric and action must have involved factors that are, at most, implicit in the written records.

Antimasonry belongs in the same category with Know Nothingism, the Red Scare, and McCarthyism. Certain behavioral characteristics are common among the members of these movements, and also similar movements throughout American history. It is part of that pattern of behavior that historian Richard Hofstadter has called "the

1

paranoid style" in American political behavior—an unreasonable fear of some group that is believed to be threatening American beliefs, values, and institutions.

To explain Antimasonry in these terms is to enter into a highly speculative realm of inquiry. The search for the psychological and socio-psychological basis of political behavior is most interesting, but at least for the historian it is inconclusive. But granting this, the task remains to examine what Antimasons said; to question why their beliefs had some appeal at one time but not at another; to discover to whom Antimasonry appealed; and to determine how it was used politically, noting what effect Antimasonry had on politics and vice versa. Ours are questions of a lesser magnitude than those raised about how Antimasonry reflects an American style of behavior or how it is characteristic of such a style in a particular era. But ours are questions for which we have the materials to construct a reasonable set of answers, and perhaps in answering these questions we will have a basis for more intelligent examination of the relationship of Antimasonry to the study of the American style of political behavior. To find answers to the questions we have asked we shall begin by considering the history and the doctrines of the Masonic Fraternity and the reasons Americans of different eras offered for denouncing the Fraternity. Since the Masonic Fraternity underwent two significant attacks in America, we can begin by comparing the phenomena in the 1790's—when it attracted little support—with the widespread interest in the post-Morgan era. We will compare the general conditions of each age, the content and quality of the written attacks on the Fraternity, and the organization into a national movement of what began as a mere sentiment against Masonry.

The origins of Freemasonry are unknown. Evidence points to the existence of a stonemasons' society that began in the fifteenth century, but the exact date of its origin and the nature of the society remain a mystery. Modern freemasonry was founded in England at the beginning of the eighteenth century. Though it would be of interest to relate the full history of the organization, it is doubtful that the modern movement had much in common with its predecessor except in one respect—the secrecy that surrounded the society.

The English Masons were devoted to social reform, which they believed could be accomplished by men who were guided by reason and imbued with a spirit of philanthropy. In this respect they reflected the Age of Enlightenment. But in addition to the belief that reason could correct the wrongs of society, the Fraternity offered mystery, a sense of brotherhood, and the excitement of ceremonies derived from the Orient. This combination of factors seemingly had widespread appeal among eighteenth-century Englishmen, for the Masons increased their membership rapidly and managed to attract writers and shopkeepers, politicians and artisans, nobility and commoners.

However, though the Fraternity prospered, it also aroused some opposition. The Catholic Church denounced it as a tool of atheists and revolutionaries, and even in England there were those who viewed the society as a threat to the power of both church and state. Though they attacked neither church nor state, it was apparent that Masons challenged both institutions at least by implication, by pursuing their objective of reform through reason. But if the English religious and political leaders feared the Fraternity, they did little to suppress it. Perhaps this toleration was due in part to the prestige of the members on the Fraternity's growing list and their insistence that they sought reform within the existing institutional structures. When criticism of the Fraternity was heard in England, it was based on the charge that behind the secrecy of the Fraternity the Masons were in fact engaged in immoral activity; they were not regarded as revolutionaries of any sort. In 1730 the Masons were accused in several journals of being "lewd, debauched, and blasphemous." Such criticisms followed Freemasonry from England to the American colonies.

In 1720 Henry Prince, a merchant, founded a Masonic lodge in Boston. Throughout the 1720's, Boston newspapers made frequent references to Masonry, but in most cases these references consisted of reprints from English journals. Those English editors occasionally described measures taken against the Masonic order by the Catholic Church. The American papers had no comments to make on these reports. It seems reasonable to assume that the Masonic lodges in Boston would, if anything, profit from public awareness that the Fraternity was disliked by the Catholic Church, which itself was viewed by almost all New Englanders as a menace to all Protestant societies.

The first strong attacks on Masonry in America came in New

York. As in England, they were based on the claim that the Masons were immoral. In 1737, the *New York Gazette* acknowledged the existence in the colony of Masonic lodges and, by reason of the secrecy of their ritual, assumed that they were following immoral practices. The Masonic oaths were mentioned and special note was made that "brutal death" was the punishment for breach of secrecy. Meeting behind closed doors, the taking of oaths, and the general tone of mystery made Masonry subject to suspicion and suggested to many the work of the devil. Antimasons, both in the eighteenth century and later times, always emphasized the secrecy that surrounded the Fraternity. Secrecy could always be cited as proof of something to hide, of some immoral activity, or of some conspiratorial plot.

In the same year that the *New York Gazette* made its charges, Philadelphia newspapers were also reporting that the Masons engaged in lewd and immoral practices. The attacks were touched off by an accident that occurred during what was claimed to be a Masonic initiation. The prospective brother was badly burned and died a few days later. A doctor who belonged to the Fraternity and two other members were subsequently tried and convicted of manslaughter. The description of the event in the *Pennsylvania Gazette,* edited by Benjamin Franklin, made the point that the defendants were not Masons at all but were only posing as members of the organization. With suspicion already aroused, such an incident would take on special significance as proof that all that was said about the secret society was true. It was no wonder that Franklin, who was an active Mason, sought to disassociate the Fraternity from the act.

America of the mid-eighteenth century was a land where formal religion was on the decline. Many from among the more literate and wealthier elements of society were attracted to Enlightenment ideas from England and France; deism was the religion of many prominent citizens. To those who decried this secularization such seeming violations of the traditional moral codes as the Masons were accused of perpetrating would be viewed not as isolated incidents but as evidence of a widespread growth of an anti-religious attitude. However, neither orthodox clergy nor laymen were able to mount a crusade against the Fraternity. Indeed, by the era of the American Revolution secret societies, both Masonic and others, were numerous and they counted among their members many of America's most influential men.

The Masons attained their peak of popularity in the years immediately following the war. Deism and religious free-thinking generally had gained widespread acceptance during that era. Formal church organization, already weak, was rent by the split resulting from the Revolution; religious toleration was raised high as part of the republican doctrine. There could be little hope of checking a group because of its secular nature. In addition, the Fraternity capitalized on the prestige of men like Franklin, Washington, and Lafayette, all of whom were Masons. The public became conscious of the association of these national heroes with Masonry.

Despite all this, another attack on the Fraternity was launched. The new Antimasonry, like the old, had for its spokesmen clergymen primarily, but their warning was not only of danger to the churches. The Antimasons of the 1790's declared that the Fraternity was bent on political revolution as well as religious upheaval, and it was a warning issued at a time when Americans had cause to fear for the future of their institutions and indeed their very survival as a nation.

The last years of the eighteenth century were times of trouble in America. War with France appeared almost a certainty; both France and England seemed intent on using the United States to further their own ends, and certainly neither showed much respect for the new country. In domestic affairs the controversy over foreign policy had caused serious political division, and clubs were being organized in many parts of the country to challenge the political power of the then dominant Federalist Party. Alexander Hamilton's tax program met violent resistance in the hills and mountains of western Pennsylvania where it finally required federal force to restore order. Criticism of the federal government and its officials was heard often enough to lead those in power to pass a sedition act in an attempt to silence the critics. It is no wonder that President Adams proclaimed a number of fast days on which citizens were asked to go to their churches to pray for the future of their country. In such an atmosphere, fear of conspiracy, especially one under foreign direction, might well seem credible.

It was on a fast day that one of Boston's leading Congregational ministers, Jedediah Morse, delivered a sermon in which he proclaimed that mysterious forces, associated with a group known as the Bavarian Illuminati, had taken control of the Revolution in France and the existing French government and now sought to control America. This group supposedly promoted irreligion and anarchy. As proof of his claims, Morse cited a book by John Robinson, a Presbyterian clergyman from Scotland, in which Robinson traced the activities of the Illuminati in France. He described their operations in England, where they used the Masonic Fraternity as a front, and he noted their plans to move on to America, again using the Fraternity. Was the secret society a cover for a foreign plot and were Americans implicated?

Newspapers in New England carried stories about the Illuminati. Like Morse, the editors warned of the danger of a conspiracy to overthrow the American government and, as proof, they pointed to the distressing course taken by the French Revolution. The experiment in revolution in France had failed. What at one time seemed to many Americans a revolution in the image of their own had led only to chaos. Perhaps the explanation of what had happened in France was that some group of conspirators had misdirected the French people and might well seek to undo the American experiment in republican government.

Other New England clergymen added similar warnings of the present danger. Those who attacked the Masons declared that the factors of political upheaval and religious conflict which fostered Antimasonry in Europe might also be present in America. But it was impossible to find proof of a connection between the Illuminati and the American Masons. George Washington and John Adams rejected the idea that American Masons were involved with foreign conspirators, and Morse was never able to produce evidence of such a connection. Though Morse had stimulated some Antimasonic interest, neither political party was prepared to adopt Antimasonry as a weapon to use against the other. The New England Federalists might well have profited from convincing Americans of a French plot to undermine their society, but the membership of so many prominent Federalists in the Fraternity must have made the Antimasons unwilling to pursue the subject. Democrat-Republicans, who had no desire to increase anti-French sentiment, were generally silent on the issue.

Morse was calling for a defense of orthodox religious doctrines and church influence at a time when public interest in both was at a low point. Politically, though there was widespread concern over the course of events in France and the preservation of order in America, there was no general acceptance of the notion of a contest between those who would preserve order and those who would bring anarchy. Federalist warnings that the election of Jefferson in 1800 would be followed by pillaging, rape, and the destruction of all government failed to impress many New Englanders, and certainly only a few outside that region. Admittedly, there were ills in republican society, but few saw efforts designed to reestablish orthodox religion and maintain Federalists in power as the means to correct those difficulties. Americans seemed willing to accept the claim of a foreign conspiracy but not the assumption that their fellow citizens were involved in the plot. With no available target to shoot at and no popularly held beliefs threatened, Antimasonry failed to become a crusade.

Though Americans of the late 1790's experienced what seems to be the kind of extreme anxiety that so often provides fertile ground on which movements aimed at countering supposed subversion grow, no such movement took root. One may conclude from this that although a high level of anxiety may increase the likelihood of a society's being attracted to simplistic explanations of and solutions for the problems of the time, such a development is not automatic. The crusade apparently must be sparked by some dramatic event or events to capture public attention. It must be well directed, and its leaders must offer some plausible grounds for the public to accept their crusade as a cure-all. Finally the crusaders must have a sufficient organization to channel toward some specific objectives the excitement of those their cause attracts. The Antimasons of the 1790's had an anxious people to whom they could appeal. So, too, did the Antimasons of the 1820's. But unlike their eighteenth-century predecessors, that later group succeeded in promoting a crusade against the Fraternity. Anxiety appears to have been a prerequisite for an antimasonic crusade but not the only, or perhaps even the primary, cause of it.

Since the anxiety is so important, we must establish its existence in the 1820's and indicate what caused it. In the 1820's large numbers of Americans experienced one or more of the following conditions: loss of traditional religious belief; fear that after a half century the principles for which the country was formed were dying, as the last of its original leaders died; significant economic change up or down, but in any case causing uncertainty; collapse of established political organizations; and

geographic uprooting. Politicians—Antimasons, Jacksonians, and others
—played upon anxiety. Preachers reacted to it. The press and some
literary figures reflected it in their writing.

When in 1826 Antimasonic attacks were leveled again, the American Fraternity was the target. The proof of conspiracy was based on its
activities. These new Antimasons claimed the Fraternity threatened the
spirit of religion at a time when twenty years of revivals had once
again made Americans conscious of their religious involvement. Now
the Antimasons vowed to defend a relatively new but widely accepted
theory of government whose proponents promised, through the establishment of democratic institutions and a democratic spirit, a better
world than men had ever known.

When the Antimasons insisted that once the Fraternity was destroyed Americans could be assured of the blessings of a moral and a
democratic society, they were appealing to an optimistic hope that the
Country had embarked on a course that led to an ideal society, and they
awakened a lingering fear that forces both human and divine sought
to prevent Americans from reaching that goal. If we consider the per-
suasions utilized by such active groups as the Jacksonians in politics and
the leaders of the temperance reform movements, we find the same
combination of optimism and fear as factors accounting for public acceptance of these movements. Though a minor political and social
phenomenon, Antimasonry was symptomatic of a general concern that
motivated Americans of the 1820's and 1830's to act in certain ways.
A brief examination of the Jacksonian and temperance movements may
serve to establish this general tendency of which Antimasonry was a
part.

In his message to Congress, explaining the veto of the bill to
recharter the Second Bank of the United States, Andrew Jackson said:

> If we can not at once, in injustice to interests wasted under
> improvident legislation make our Government what it ought to be,
> we can at least take a stand against all new grants of monopolies
> and exclusive privileges, against any prostitution of our Govern-
> ment to the advancement of the few at the expense of the many.

In this, as in many other passages, Jackson used language and
imagery more dramatic and extreme than a debate over economic policy

warranted. The President was declaring his action to be in the name of democracy, and he was utilizing a rhetoric that plainly was intended to impress on the American people the extreme danger of the Bank to democracy. In the face of such danger, normal political action was insufficient. To Jackson this was to be a crusade; he used the term "war." Whatever one may say about the right or wrong of Jackson's action, historians agree that his attack on the Bank was out of proportion to any possible danger from that institution. Furthermore, it has become evident from recent study that Jackson and his party were not even promoters of democracy, though they espoused democratic ideas. Indeed, by the late 1820's the political and, in many parts of the country, the economic democratization of America was well launched and without serious opposition. But the crusaders for democracy were heard often and they excited at least some of the public.

Politicians were not the only crusaders, and they were not the only crusaders to use this extreme appeal when no real danger, no real enemy, in fact, existed. So, for example, temperance advocates carried their calls to end drinking to the point of a crusade though there was no evidence that drunkenness had increased or become a major social problem. The enemy was the liquor dealer, that agent of the Devil who sought to destroy Americans. This crusade, like the political ones, had a specific object, a target that could be identified and eliminated. It promised great rewards once that target was crushed, and it called for immediate and, if necessary, extreme action to accomplish the objective. Having accomplished their purpose the crusaders declared that Americans would have the opportunity to enjoy the fruits of a rich land, a free political system, and a morally directed society upon which God looked with great favor.

Though separation of church and state was affirmed in the Constitution, and though by 1826 only Massachusetts still maintained a formal church-state relationship, the place of religion in American society was a matter of debate and of widespread discussion. The minister and reform leader Lyman Beecher accepted the separation of church and state without concern but insisted that such a separation only made more urgent the need to establish Christian principles. Beecher assumed, and many Americans agreed with him, that a Christian society was a moral society and that if America was to fulfill its God-directed mission to become the most perfect society the world had known, it had to be moral. Church and state might be separate but that did not sanction the secularization of society. The secular and religious spheres were to remain one, and the plethora of crusades provided evidence of the widespread acceptance of that unity.

Antimasonry was such a crusade. The Antimasons merged moral and secular concerns. They viewed a threat to morality as a threat to all aspects of American life. They defended morality for the sake of democracy, the key secular characteristic of that life; and when they became a political force, they defended democracy for the sake of morality. They recognized no separation of those spheres. But convincing Americans that the Masonic Fraternity was immoral and undemocratic was difficult, for the Fraternity had a history of promoting morality and, in America, many of the country's most respected men, and indeed its national heroes, were members. The Antimasonic crusade attracted support only in a few places where religious, economic, and political conditions combined to make both the general public and the politicians receptive to the ideas of such a crusade. But we must remember that Antimasonry was only one of the many crusades in which Americans of this era participated.

The Antimasonic movement began in the hills and valleys of that part of New York State that, as historian Whitney Cross reminds us, was called the "burned over district," because of the numerous religious revivals and reform crusades that were conducted in the region in the years from 1825 to 1850. But if the special conditions of western New York made its population susceptible to Antimasonry, it appealed to other segments of American society for other reasons, for the crusade spread to other parts of New York and to the New England States, as well as to Pennsylvania, Ohio, and other Northwestern states. It attracted a following in urban New York and Boston as well as in towns, villages, and countrysides. In other words, it is difficult to find reasons for the interest in Antimasonry. Nevertheless, we will suggest some possible answers.

Professional politicians aside, Antimasonry attracted people who were involved in reform movements and religious crusades, and those people came from many places and had diverse backgrounds. One would be hard-pressed to prove a relation between moral concern and geographic, economic, or social origins of the concerned parties. What we can offer as a generalization is that Antimasons were especially concerned about the level of morality; all who shared this strong moral concern were not Antimasons but all Antimasons were moralists. It is evident that Antimasons were often members of evangelically inclined religious groups since participating in a moral crusade would seem proper in the eyes of evangelical clergy. But evangelical religion was widespread in this age, and often urban-centered, as well as the rural, interest existed in such religious practice.

While Antimasonic rhetoric was crowded with moralizing, it was often coupled with expressions of the desire to see equal rights, equal opportunity, and a spirit of social equality protected. As was the case with the Jacksonians, this was a democratic rhetoric but did not reflect an effort to promote democracy. New York City's Antimasonic leader, Henry Ward, claimed that "the sturdy yeoman, the vigorous mechanic, the honest countryman, are the materials of the party." But there is evidence that Antimasonic ranks were filled by people from all classes and that, though in broad terms the crusaders coupled morality with democracy, proponents were not necessarily those who were less than equal. The rhetoric of egalitarian democracy was common to all parties and was more or less appealing to Americans in general and not to one class of society. Antimasons were to be found among the rich, the city residents, and the prominent as well as among those whom Ward describes.

Finally in the case of receptivity to the Antimasonic party, as contrasted to interest in the crusade, the particular condition of state politics was important. As the historian Richard McCormick argues, in states where political party lines were unclear, the Antimasonic party was strongest. Thus, as one example, Vermont had no coherent party system in this era, and Antimasonry became a major political force; while in neighboring New Hampshire there were strong party organizations, and Antimasonry had little importance in that state's politics. Put simply, Antimasonry was significant where politicians and public were not already committed to some other political organization.

If the realities of self-interest made a man an Antimason, the crusade in which he participated was never proclaimed to have been launched for the sake of that interest. Most Antimasons, like most people engaged in any crusade, could not sort out and distinguish the self-interested from the selfless factors that had led them to participate in the crusade. They could not identify the real conflict from the imagined one. That confusion is probably both the strength and the weakness of a crusade. Antimasonry began among people with very real concerns, and it began with a very real event, but the sense of reality was always being submerged in the rhetoric of selfless crusade against a foe, whose great strength and evil motives were the product of the Antimason's imagination. In presenting the history of Antimasonic activity we begin with a real and dramatic event, the Morgan case. No matter how Antimasons chose to attack the Fraternity, invariably they cited this incident as proof of their claim.

The Morgan disappearance—and soon it was presumed, murder—attracted widespread attention. The kidnappers were identified and brought to trial but were acquitted. The verdict aroused protest, especially when it was noted that the judge and most of the jury were Masons. At first it seemed a case of conspiracy among members of a fraternal group to protect their brothers. Those who wrote against the Fraternity, most of them friends of Morgan, argued that the testimony given at the trial was sufficient to have convicted the accused Masons. Since they were freed, the assumption was that the Masons had subverted justice. To the Antimasons, all this proved that the crime was not just the work of a few irresponsible Masons, as the Fraternity claimed, but the fraternal organization as a whole.

The Morgan incident prompted further investigation into the role of the Masonic Fraternity. Antimasons discovered that though the number of Masons in the state was relatively small, they held most of the high judicial and political positions in the state; moreover, many clergymen belonged to the Fraternity. But if such association were to imply some sort of guilt, the Fraternity, and not just one group of Masons, had to be shown to be evil. The conflict was transferred into a dramatic struggle of good and evil, and reality gave way. In many towns and villages public pressure was exerted to disband the Masonic lodges and a number of Antimasonic newspapers were founded to spread the story of the Fraternity's supposed crime.

Antimasons invariably began their criticism of the Fraternity by pointing to its secret rituals, those rituals that Morgan would have exposed and that the Masons considered so important that they silenced him. Secrecy, the Antimasons claimed, implied that there was something to hide. They related the words *secret* and *darkness* and even noted that much of the Masonic ritual was conducted in the dark. And darkness, they reminded their audiences, was the realm of the "Prince of Darkness," the Devil. But what were the Devil's objectives? One answer, of course, was that he sought to undermine religion. Using much the same accusations that Morse and Dwight had leveled, the Antimasons cited the stories of the Bavarian Illuminati, that secret group of atheists who wished to destroy Protestantism. The Antimasons claimed that politically the Illuminati sought to destroy republican government, putting in its place either a monarchy, with the monarch inspired by the Devil, or they sought to produce anarchy. Economic freedom was to give way to a closed society in which the Masons controlled all wealth and would use that wealth to serve the purposes of the Devil.

In the first year or two of Antimasonic agitation the case against the Fraternity was presented as a crusade against evil forces that threatened the moral quality of society and endangered the spirit of democracy. The crusaders were attracted by the opportunity to participate actively in such a movement, just as they would be attracted to many other crusades whose purpose was also to attack the Devil and preserve democracy. Their opponent was the Masonic Fraternity but, interestingly, not the individual Mason. Had Antimasons denounced Masons, the movement would have become a war of one element of society against another. By assuming that the Fraternity was an agency of the Devil, that it was a secret conspiracy, cloaked in darkness, the Antimasons could claim that members of the Fraternity were duped into joining and that once the darkness was dispelled these Masons would abandon the Fraternity and, indeed, many did just that. Most of the early Antimasonic tracts were designed to expose the origins and supposed true purposes of Masonry. The word *light* appeared often in those tracts. In some cases, groups of Masons were singled out for special warning and presented with Antimasonic arguments. Thus, a group of prominent laymen addressed those clergymen who belonged to the Fraternity, arguing that Masonry was of the Devil. If the clergymen recanted, presumably they would remain in the good graces of those who attacked the Fraternity. Indeed, large numbers of Masons seceded from the Fraternity and played an active role in the Antimasonic crusade. After all, who better could expose the evils of Masonry and its dangers than one who had been sucked in?

With the Devil as the enemy and the Fraternity as his agent, a crusade against Masonry provided those who engaged in it the opportunity to work actively to fulfill God's will and to protect those beliefs and institutions which they held sacred. But once Antimasonry became political, the conflict became more personal. Men were either with you or against you; opponents had to be singled out and attacked.

It was easy to become impatient with the process of converting Masons. If the Masons, even after being shown the light, refused to leave the Fraternity, it must be proof that they were evil, that they used the Fraternity to further their own economic interest, to acquire and unfairly hold political power, to make the law work especially for them, and to defy the moral codes to which the rest of society adhered. The Devil was behind these men, but they were culpable and must be stopped and in some way punished. The courts could deal with them if they broke the law; but because of their oaths, so Antimasons claimed, they protected one another, and it was difficult to punish Masonic criminals. The Morgan case had proved that. Even if evidence were gathered, Masons controlled the courts. The judges were Masons and politicians appointed the judges. If the Masons dominated the economy and closed off opportunity could this grip be broken? Economic power could be related to political power in many ways. If the Masons dominated political offices could they be ousted? The political system was so structured that only a party organization and concerted party effort could break that hold and reform the political system so that in the future the people could control politics. Everything pointed to Antimasonic efforts being devoted to political action. Public opinion had to be aroused and then channeled into a party, a weapon, to use against the Masons. The ballot box, the democratic system, must be employed if morality and the institutions and spirit of democracy were to be preserved.

In attacking the Fraternity through politics the Antimasons, hoping to preserve the character of a crusade, based their attack on the principle of defense and furtherance of democracy. Masons were now labelled as aristocrats, monopolists, and self-interested individuals who lacked either interest in or respect for democratic principles. The delegates to the first Antimasonic party convention in New York used the format of the Declaration of Independence in proclaiming their grievances against the Fraternity. As a political organization they utilized a convention system in choosing their candidates and so could claim to be following a democratic procedure in which the people chose the candidate.

For a time the Antimasonic crusade functioned successfully as a political force. In Jabbez Hammond's *History of New York Politics,* written in 1846, a former Antimason noted that in local elections in towns and villages of western New York, politicians who had held office for long periods of time—but who were Masons—were suddenly ousted from office. We know that politicians such as Samuel Southwick in New York and Martin Flint in Vermont made significant political comebacks gaining support seemingly for no reason other than their new Antimasonic stance. As a party, the Antimasons won control of Vermont politics and made a quick and strong showing in New York and Pennsylvania. Since the Antimasons lacked organization these political victories must be attributed entirely to public excitement over the crusade against the Fraternity. But, as we have noted, that excitement was a local phenomenon, great in one area of a state but not in others and limited entirely to a few northern states. The politicians who directed the party had ambitions of attaining statewide and even national power. They had to do more than just ride the wave of Antimasonic fervor.

The Antimasonic party became more than an arm of the Antimasonic crusade. In order to understand politicians' interest in Antimasonry, discounting their possible dedication to the cause of destroying the Fraternity, we must consider why they might create such a party. This is a particularly complex problem involving the nature of politics at both the state and the national level and the relation between state and national politics in the late 1820's and early 1830's. It would require more space than could be given in this essay and would carry us beyond the proper realm of study of the Antimasonic crusade to attempt a detailed explanation of these political developments, but it is useful in following the history of the crusade to consider the subject, even if briefly and necessarily superficially.

It is evident from the pre-election confusion and the presence of four candidates contesting for the presidency in 1824 that the Democratic-Republican Party had ceased to function as a party. With the demise of that Party the country was left without national parties. To some politicians Antimasonry appeared as a basis on which to build a new party, as to others the personality of Andrew Jackson was a

basis for such organization. It is evident that such Antimasonic leaders
as Thurlow Weed, William Seward, Francis Granger, and William
Wirt, who became the party's first and only candidate for President,
were interested in far more than the destruction of the Fraternity,
though they recited the language of a crusade.

On the state level the opportunities for a new party varied from
state to state as Richard McCormick has demonstrated. In states where
a strong two party system operated, interest in an Antimasonic party
was absent. Thus, even in areas of the Northeast, such as Massachusetts and New Hampshire, where the crusade had attracted interest,
we find no evidence of significant Antimasonic political support. On
the other hand in New York, Pennsylvania, and Vermont, where the
state party system was either weak or badly splintered, Antimasonic
parties were organized and strong. But state political organizations
needed some tie to national politics as a means of attracting voter
interest and support. Martin Van Buren, for example, after 1826 was
able to weld together a strong state party in New York thanks in
large measure to his support and association with Andrew Jackson.
Van Buren men were Jackson men. In part because Jackson refused
to reject his Masonic affiliation, the Antimasons were unwilling to
support him in 1828 and instead backed no candidate, though inform-
ally they worked for John Quincy Adams, who had renounced the
Fraternity. But not all supporters of Adams were Antimasons; and on
the state level in New York, Antimasons opposed an Adams man in the
contest for Governor. Antimasonic leaders faced the problem of going
it alone or of forming a coalition with Masons who were also Adams
men. They chose the former route, which kept something of the
crusade quality alive in Antimasonry. But they prevented the party from
becoming strong, and by splintering the vote in all three states where
the Antimasons were well organized, they caused the Jackson men to
triumph in each. In the years after 1828, only in Vermont was crusade
excitement strong enough to produce statewide control, and only
Vermont cast its electoral votes for the Antimasonic candidate for
President in 1832.

The election of 1832 marked the end of the Antimasonic party,
though evidence of Antimasonic sentiment remained for many years.
The party leaders again faced the problem of acquiring a national
association or maintaining the image of the crusade. In this instance

the situation was more difficult than in 1828 for both Presidential candidates, Jackson and Clay, were avowed Masons. For the Antimasons to have backed either one would have meant the end of any connection between the party and the crusade. William Seward in his address to the National Antimasonic Convention in 1830 and in his speech before the New York State Legislature in 1831 made clear the decision of the party leaders: they would follow the crusade and reject the candidates. The Party chose its own candidate, William Wirt, and went down to total defeat. The crusade, which was to have provided the basis for a national political party, had instead hamstrung the politicians and led nowhere. Meantime, the crusade itself had lost its impetus. Many fraternal groups had disbanded in the areas where the crusade excitement had run high and so the object of the crusade was partly attained. As evidence of the decline in interest in Antimasonry and the diverting of interest to other concerns, an examination of the *Anti-Masonic Enquirer,* published in Rochester, reveals frequent references to the Fraternity until 1830, but then, having identified Masons and Jackson men as one in the same, the paper's editor discussed a proposed canal tax, the abolition of imprisonment for debt, the Bank, the tariff, and all other major political issues of the day. The enemy had become the Democrats not the Masons. By 1832 the Fraternity was all but ignored.

But the failure of the Antimasonic party and the declining interest in the crusade do not prove that Americans of that era were unresponsive to crusades, or that American politicians would have been wise to avoid relating their political activities to them. As we have noted the Jacksonians were crusaders. They, too, claimed to fight for democracy, first against the supposed aristocratic presidential candidate John Quincy Adams, and then against the supposed agent of foreign and aristocratic interest, the Bank. As we have noted, in many respects reformers of that era crusaded for democracy and they, like the Jacksonians, attracted widespread support. Perhaps the Antimasons' problem was that the object of their crusade was too specific: either you were or you were not a Mason. There could be no middle ground, no compromise with Masons for the sake of allowing various political forces. Also the Fraternity was too well entrenched both because of its long history as an agent rejecting class distinction, expressing concern for one's fellow human beings, and in general promoting progress through the pursuit of knowledge and the performance of good works, and because the Fraternity counted too many respected, even revered men among its members. Even if you could believe that Jackson and Clay might be part of an antidemocratic, anti-Christian conspiracy, could Franklin, Washington, and LaFayette, who was greeted with almost universal praise when he revisited America in 1826, have also had such evil designs or been so naive as to have been duped into supporting an organization with such un-American objectives? To most Americans it seemed unlikely.

The history of Antimasonry is but one chapter in the history of crusades in this decade. It suggests that Americans were both fearful and optimistic, convinced they were menaced by forces that would destroy their society, and determined to identify and eliminate those forces. That such a crusade might serve one's self-interest was obviously important and helps explain why an individual became an Antimason, but like all crusaders, Antimasons were not in the movement simply for self-serving reasons; no crusade in any age can be explained by looking solely for that sort of interest. Rather, we must recognize that the crusade developed because at least some Americans found a cause that went beyond self-interest without endangering—and perhaps by even furthering—that interest. The crusade was characterized by fervor, excitement, extremism, and determination that no movement based on self-interest could display. Americans of the 1820's and 1830's, and at times since, have shown a great propensity to be attracted by crusades. It has given our politics a sense of urgency and excitement that defies explanation if one were simply to examine the issues debated, and it has led to the creation of reform movements more numerous and with objectives more urgently sought than the reasoned examination of the need for reform in America would lead us to expect. In a society where secular practices and institutions are cloaked in a religious mystique the crusade has come to characterize organized efforts of all sorts and for the purpose of accomplishing a great variety of objectives.

source 1

The Danger of Conspiracy

Jedediah Morse

In this sermon Jedediah Morse, by recounting the history of the rise of natural religion in Europe and its relation to the overthrow of governments, sought to establish the existing danger to American government if the forces of atheism were left unchecked. His story is of a secret group which, he claimed, took over the once harmless Masonic societies of Europe and turned them into agents of revolution and irreligion. Nothing was sacred, nothing safe from attack by these men who hid behind the secret workings and respectability of the Masonic order. Morse concludes with the warning that these men are at work in many countries, including America.

About the year 1728, Voltaire, so celebrated for his wit and brilliancy, and not less distinguished for his hatred of christianity and his abandonment of principle, formed a systematical design to destroy christianity, and to introduce in its stead a general diffusion of irreligion and atheism. For this purpose he associated with himself Frederic the II, king of Prussia, and Mess. D'Alembert and Diderot, the principal compilers of the Encyclopedie; all men of talents, atheists, and in the like manner abandoned. The principal parts of this system were:

1. The compilation of the Encyclopedie; in which with great art and insidiousness the doctrines of Natural as well as Christian Theology were rendered absurd and ridiculous; and the mind of the reader was insensibly steeled against conviction and duty.

Jedediah Morse, "Dangers and Duties of Citizens of the United States," Collected Political Sermons (Princeton, N.J.: Princeton University Library), I, pp. 10–14.

2. The overthrow of the religious orders in Catholic countries; a step essentially necessary to the destruction of the religion professed in those countries.

3. The establishment of a sect of philosophists to serve, it is presumed, as a conclave, a rallying point, for all their followers.

4. The appropriation to themselves, and their disciples, of the places and honours of members of the French Academy, the most respectable literary society in France, and always considered as containing none but men of prime learning and talents. In this way they designed to hold out themselves, and their friends, as the only persons of great literary and intellectual distinction in that country, and to dictate all literary opinions to the nation.

5. The fabrication of Books of all kinds against christianity, especially such as excite doubt, and generate contempt and derision. Of these they issued, by themselves and their friends, who early became numerous, an immense number; so printed, as to be purchased for little or nothing, and so written, as to catch the feelings, and steal upon the approbation, of every class of men.

6. The formation of a secret Academy, of which Voltaire was the standing president, and in which books were formed, altered, forged, imputed as post-humous to deceased writers of reputation, and sent abroad with the weight of their names. These were printed and circulated, at the lowest price, through all classes of men, in an uninterrupted succession, and through every part of the kingdom.

Nor were the labours of this Academy confined to religion. They attacked also morality and government, unhinged gradually the minds of men, and destroyed their reverence for every thing heretofore esteemed sacred.

In the meantime, the Masonic Societies, which had been originally instituted for convivial and friendly purposes only, were, especially in France and Germany, made the professed scenes of debate concerning religion, morality, and government, by these philosophists, who had in great numbers become Masons. For such debate the legalized existence of Masonry, its profound secrecy, its solemn and mystic rites and symbols, its mutual correspondence, and its extension through most civilized countries, furnished the greatest advantages. All here was free, safe, calculated to encourage the boldest excursions of restless opinion and impatient ardour, and to make and fix the deepest impressions. Here, and in no other place, under such arbitrary governments, could every innovator in these important subjects utter every sentiment, however daring, and attack every doctrine and institution, however guarded by law or sanctity. In the secure and unrestrained debates of the lodge, every novel, licentious, and alarming opinion was resolutely advanced. Minds, already tinged with philosophism, were here speedily blackened with a deep and deadly dye; and those, which came fresh and innocent to the scene of contamination, became early and irremediably corrupted. A stubborn incapacity of conviction, and a flinty insensibility to every moral and natural tie, grew of course out of this combination of causes; and men were surely prepared, before themselves were aware, for every plot and perpetration. In these hot beds were sown the seeds of that astonishing Revolution, and all its dreadful appendages, which now spreads dismay and horror throughout half the globe.

While these measures were advancing the great design with a regular and rapid progress, Doctor Adam Weishaupt, professor of the Canon law in the University of Ingolstadt, a city of Bavaria (in Germany) formed, about the year 1777, the order of Illuminati. This order is professedly a higher order of Masons, originated by himself, and grafted on ancient Masonic Institutions. The secrecy, solemnity, mysticism, and correspondence of Masonry, were in this new order preserved and enhanced; while the ardour of innovation, the impatience of civil and moral restraints, and the aims against government, morals, and religion, were elevated, expanded, and rendered more systematical, malignant, and daring.

In the societies of Illuminati doctrines were taught, which strike at the root of all human happiness and virtue; and every such doctrine was either expressly or implicitly involved in their system.

The being of God was denied and ridiculed.

Government was asserted to be a curse, and authority a mere usurpation.

Civil society was declared to be the only apostasy of man.

The possession of property was pronounced to be robbery.

Chastity and natural affection were declared to be nothing more than groundless prejudices.

Adultery, assassination, poisoning, and other crimes of the like infernal nature, were taught as lawful, and even as virtuous actions.

To crown such a system of falsehood and horror all means were declared to be lawful, provided the end was good.

In this last doctrine men are not only loosed from every bond, and from every duty; but from every inducement to perform any thing which is good, and, abstain from any thing which is evil; and are set upon each other, like a company of hellhounds to worry, rend, and destroy. Of the goodness of the end every man is to judge for himself; and most men, and all men who resemble the Illuminati, will pronounce every end to be good, which will gratify their inclinations. The great and good ends proposed by the Illuminati, as the ultimate objects of their union, are the overthrow of religion, government, and human society—civil and domestic. These they pronounce to be so good, that murder, butchery, and war, however extended and dreadful, are declared by them to be completely justifiable, if necessary for these great purposes. With such an example in view, it will be in vain to hunt for ends, which can be evil.

Correspondent with this summary was the whole system. No villainy, no impiety, no cruelty, can be named, which was not vindicated; and no virtue, which was not covered with contempt.

The means by which this society was enlarged, and its doctrines spread, were of every promising kind. With unremitted ardour and diligence the members insinuated themselves into every place of power and trust, and into every literary, political and friendly society; engrossed as much as possible the education of youth, especially of distinction; became licensers of the press, and directors of every literary journal; waylaid every foolish prince, every unprincipled civil officer, and every abandoned clergyman; entered boldly into the desk, and with unhallowed hands, and satanic lips, polluted the pages of God; enlisted in their service almost all the booksellers, and of course the printers, of Germany; inundated the country with books, replete with infidelity, irreligion, immorality, and obscenity; prohibited the printing, and prevented the sale, of books of the contrary character; decried and ridiculed them when published in spite of their efforts; panegyrized and trumpeted those of themselves and their coadjutors; and in a word made more numerous, more diversified, and more strenuous exertions, than an active imagination would have preconceived.

To these exertions their success has been proportioned. Multitudes of the Germans, notwithstanding the gravity, steadiness, and sobriety of their national character, have become either partial or entire converts to these wretched doctrines; numerous societies have been established among them; the public faith and morals have been unhinged; and the political and religious affairs of that empire have assumed an aspect, which forebodes its total ruin. In France, also, Illuminatism has been eagerly and extensively adopted; and those men, who have had, successively, the chief direction of the public affairs of that country, have been members of this society. Societies have also been erected in Switzerland and Italy, and have contributed probably to the success of the French, and to the overthrow of religion and government, in those countries. Mentz was delivered up to Custine by the Illuminati; and that General appears to have been guillotined, because he declined to encourage the same treachery with respect to Manheim.

Nor have England and Scotland escaped the contagion. Several societies have been erected in both of those countries. Nay in the private papers, seized in the custody of the leading members in Germany, several such societies are recorded as having been erected in America, before the year 1786.

It is a remarkable fact, that a large proportion of the sentiments, here stated, have been publicly avowed and applauded in the French legislature. The being and providence of God have been repeatedly denied and ridiculed. Christ has been mocked with the grossest insult. Death, by a solemn legislative decree has been declared to be an eternal sleep. Marriage has been degraded to a farce, and the community, by the law of divorce, invited to universal prostitution. In the school of public instruction atheism is professedly taught; and at an audience before the legislature, Nov. 30, 1793, the head scholar declared, that he and his schoolfellows detested a God; a declaration received by the members with unbounded applause, and rewarded with the fraternal kiss of the president, and with the honors of the fitting.

source 2

Adams Responds to
the Antimasonic Attacks

John Adams

Though quite willing to believe the worst about the activities of secret revolutionary societies in France, President Adams refused to accept Morse's claim that Americans would join in a plot against their government. Perhaps there was a conspiracy at work in America but, Adams insisted, it was a foreign conspiracy. George Washington, a Mason of long standing though not active for many years, shared Adams' view. When Washington died in 1799, the Masons were prominent participants in his funeral, making sure the public was aware of his membership in the Fraternity.

With such prominent Americans and Federalists publicly rejecting the idea of an American Masonic plot, and with Morse lacking evidence of his charge, he had little chance of exciting widespread public opinion against the Fraternity.

July 1798

To the Freemasons of the State of Maryland
GENTLEMEN,

I thank you for this generous and noble address.

The zeal you display to vindicate your society from the imputations and suspicions of being "inemical to regular government and divine religion," is greatly to your honor. It has been an opinion of many considerate men, as long as I can remember, that your society might, in some time or other, be made an instrument of danger and disorder to the world. Its ancient existence and universal prevalence are good proofs that it has not heretofore been applied to mischievous

Charles F. Adams, *The Works of John Adams* (Boston: Little, Brown, 1854), XIV, pp. 212–31.

purposes; and in this country I presume that no one has *attempted* to employ it for purposes foreign from its *original* institution. But in an age and in countries where *morality* is, by such members, considered as mere *convenience,* and *religion* a *lie,* you are better judges than I am, whether ill uses have been or may be made of Masonry.

Your appeal to my own breast, and your declaration that I shall *there* find your sentiments, I consider as a high compliment; and feel a pride in perceiving and declaring that the opinions, principles, and feelings expressed are conformable to my own. With you, I fear that no hope remains but in preparation for the worst that may ensue.

Persevere, gentlemen, in revering the Constitution which secures your liberties, in loving your country, in practising the *social* as well as the *moral* duties, in presenting your lives with those of your fellow-citizens, a barrier to defend your independence, and may the architect all-powerful surround you with walls impregnable, and receive you, finally (your country, happy, prosperous, and glorious), to mansions eternal in the Heavens? . . .

JOHN ADAMS

The Morgan Case and the Proof of an Internal Conspiracy

Committee on the Abduction of William Morgan

When Antimasonry was revived nearly 30 years later, its proponents built their case, not on some foreign danger, though they repeated the story of the Illuminati and declared it to be involved, but on an incident which they claimed proved the conspirators were Americans at work in America. The Morgan story was told and retold both at the time it occurred and for years thereafter. Not only did it supposedly prove Masons would murder to keep their activities secret but it led to all sorts of speculation as to who the Masons were and what they intended to do. The demand to get at the true nature of the Fraternity and to uncover its real objectives culminated in an investigation conducted by a committee of the New York State Senate in 1829. Though the report indicted the Masons on many counts and called for legislation against the Fraternity, none was forthcoming. But the Senate's findings only confirmed what others had said for the preceding three years, and Antimasons had already sought to check the Fraternity in other ways.

At no period since the revolution has the public mind been as severely agitated as by the abduction and subsequent unhappy fate of William Morgan. The great moral shock has been felt with few exceptions, by people of every age, sex and condition. The high-handed violation of all law, the great number concerned in it, the cheerless and desolate condition of his bereaved wife and children, the uncertainty that for a while attended the whole affair, were all calculated to arouse the public mind to an unexampled state of sympathy, indignation and abhorrence. But these passions, although intense at that

Report of the Committee on the Abduction of William Morgan made to the Senate, February 14, 1829 (Albany, 1829). This tract is to be found in the Benno Loewy Collection of the Cornell University Library.

period, are in their nature evanescent, and before this time would have spent their force, had not the attempt to bring the offenders to the bar of justice produced a development of facts, circumstances, and principles as lasting in their effects as the love of liberty in man.

. . .

The people of this state are distinguished by their attachment to a pure administration of justice as connected with the trial by jury— by their love of self-government, and by their aversion to everything which directly or indirectly tends to thwart the operation of the democratic principles, which are the basis of our political compact. They are distinguished by their jealousy of powerful and talented men, and especially of the combinations of such men for purposes either unknown or known to affect improperly the even and healthful current of our political affairs. They have learned that concentration of feeling, of interest, and of effort are to the moral and political what the lever and the screw are to the mechanical powers, and they dread their operation.

The order of the Jesuits, whose discipline secured unity of design and secrecy in action—which used the solemn sanctions of the most high God to subserve purposes the most selfish and profane, presented to the 16th century a moral power greater than the world had ever known. It penetrated with the silence and certainty of fate, the secrets of every court in Europe, and subjugated, without the force of arms, one half of the continent of America to the dominion of the Pope. This order has been crushed, but within the last 120 years another has arisen—the society of free and accepted masons.

This institution, professing to be of ancient and even of divine origin, adopting sanctions similar to those of the order of the Jesuits, and commanding a secrecy still more profound, have recently made demonstrations of a power, astonishing in its effects upon the social and political compact, and of a character such as the friends of free institutions cannot fail to deplore.

The powers manifested by the masonic institution which may have been exercised in its unlawful restraints of human liberty, or pretended jurisdiction over human life, are not now so much the occasion of alarm as its fearful moral influence, exerted upon the public press, and its facility in controlling results in the tribunals of justice. The public feeling at the West, which has borne the ridicule and sarcasm of those interested in quelling it, is not, as they would have it believed, the mere animal sensation indicated by brutes, whose bellowings mark the spot where some victim has been slaughtered; but is the result of sober, calculating reflection, looking to causes and their consequences; to existing evils and the remedies to be applied; to posterity, and not the present generation alone. The life of one man, or even a thousand, in a republic consisting of 12,000,000 inhabitants, politically considered, is of but little moment. But that the streams of justice should flow pure and uncontaminated is matter of infinite concern not only to the people of the West but to the whole state; not only to the state, but the Union.

But they have lost the confidence they formerly reposed in the tribunals of justice. They believe that masonry exerts its influence in civil as well as criminal cases; in arbitrations, references, and in trials by jury, before justices of the peace, as well as in the higher courts. Formerly from one half to two thirds of their justices belonged to the fraternity of masons—now not one in twenty are of the initiated; and this change has been chiefly produced by their entire conviction of the fact that masonry pervades and influences the courts of justice.

During what have been called the Morgan trials, and other civil cases which owe their origin to his abduction and subsequent fate, the people have crowded the courts of justice to overflowing. They have watched the deportment of masonic witnesses upon the stand; some of whom, of good repute in society, have sworn to facts, which in the opinion of by-standers, were not credited by a single one of the hundreds of persons who were present. It is believed that grand juries, a majority of whom were masons, have omitted to find bills of indictment when there was proof before them of outrages, not surpassed in grossness and indecency by any committed in the country since its first settlement. Those outrages were committed upon a mason, who had been in the daily habit of exposing in lectures what were once called the secrets of masonry. Grand jurymen have said, while assembled for the discharge of their duties and when it was apprehended their masonic brethren would be implicated, "we must not let our brethren suffer." In a case of recent occurrence, a defendant who had been sued by a mason, not willing to have his case tried by masonic jurymen, challenged them; stating to the court his readiness to prove the character of the masonic oaths and to show that the obligations assumed by them were of a description unfitting them to sit in judgment between the parties; and of such a nature as to disqualify them in point of law. With the assent of the circuit judge, the masonic jurymen left the box, and the trial proceeded. The counsel for the defendant entertained, no doubt upon the law and the facts he could prove, that the challenges were well taken.

The committee might multiply cases of this description, but they are omitted for others of more public notoriety, and tending to the same point. The case of Col. King is one fully known to the public, and partly from information contained in his newspaper communications. The committee therefore recur to it, the more readily, but without any intention of expressing an opinion of his innocence or guilt. He had been suspected of having had a concern in some of the transactions affecting William Morgan. He went to Washington in the fall or winter of 1826–27; applied for public employment, and obtained, with the assistance of some of his masonic friends, the place of sutler to the U.S. troops in the territory of Arkansas. The suspicions resting upon the public mind in regard to him increased; and Messrs. Garlinghouse and Bates were despatched by the Governor of this state, for the purpose of arresting him, and perhaps some others, who were supposed to be fugitives from justice. They ascertained that King was at Cantonment Towson, and procured an order from the Secretary at War, to the commander to surrender him forthwith. The fruit of this sovereign exercise of the state and United States power, in procuring the return of this humble sutler to answer in the courts of this state for the misdemeanors charged upon him, was precisely such as might have been anticipated upon the supposition that the obligations of masons to each other, are such as they undoubtedly must be, upon the proof that has been presented to the public. Bound to protect each other by the tenor of obligations in their view of higher import than those they owe to the state or country which gives them protection, the officer of the Fort, instead of obeying the order of the Secretary at War, notified King of his danger; and Garlinghouse and Bates soon found by the escape of King that their labors, arduous as they had been, were defeated by the machinations of masonry.

The annals of criminal jurisprudence furnish no parallel in many respects to the case of William Morgan. The majesty of the laws and the powers of masonry have been brought into conflict. What may be the result of the mighty struggle none can tell. But the events of the last two years during which the conflict has been maintained, induce the belief that masonry will be victorious. The history of Morgan's fate is short and simple: On the 11th day of September, 1826, he was taken by several masons in broad day, by force, from the village of Batavia to Canandaigua, a distance of 50 miles, and there upon a process originated for the occasion, confined in jail. While on his way from Batavia, one of his kidnappers who had him in charge, said with an oath, Morgan should not be taken from him alive. After a short confinement in the prison at Canandaigua, he was taken out on Sunday the 12th, at evening, and amidst his distressing cries of murder, was forced into a post coach. He was then driven through a densely populated country, 110 miles to the United States Fort on the Niagara river, and there confined. The horses and coaches used in conveying him from Canandaigua were owned or procured by masons. And the owner of a livery stable then kept at Rochester, who at that time and now is a royal arch mason, actually charged the Grand Chapter for the use of his coaches and horses to Lewiston. Pains were taken to obtain masonic drivers. The last driver, however, accidentally was not a mason. It was Corydon Fox. He drove the prisoner, attended by three masons, to the graveyard about 80 rods distant from the Fort and was directed to halt. The party dismounted, and Fox was told to return to Lewiston. This was in the night time. Shortly after, Fox made some observations about his trip to the Fort, which excited fears in the minds of the brotherhood, and within a short period, a special lodge was called, and Fox was initiated as a member of it. An unusual number of masons were at Lewiston and in the vicinity of the Fort during the three or four days of Morgan's confinement there, and nightly visited the Fort. The sufferings of Morgan were probably terminated on the night of the 18th of September, 1826.

Morgan was fifty years old; in point of talents and manners was above mediocrity—had fought in the defence of his country at the battle of New Orleans, and immediately preceding his abduction from Batavia had unfortunately for himself and family been concerned in writing a book upon masonry, disclosing its usages, oaths, and obligations.

It has been fully established by the testimony in the various trials that have been had, that a great number of masons have been directly or indirectly concerned in the abduction and subsequent fate of Morgan. But notwithstanding the publicity of this transaction arising from the great number necessarily concerned in it—notwithstanding the thousands of dollars offered as rewards by the executive of this state, as well as the governor of Canada, to those who would give information of his fate, and the thousands contributed and expended by humane and patriotic citizens to ferret out the iniquity; and notwithstanding, too, a commissioner has been sent by the legislature to add his talents and industry to that of the courts in the country, still no record tells us whose hands have been stained with the blood of this masonic victim.

The committee assume the fact that the life of Morgan has been destroyed; and they are compelled to do so from the irresistible weight of circumstances tending to fortify that conviction. The love of gold, incited by the great rewards which have been offered; the love of character stimulating individuals implicated, and indeed the fair fame of whole classes of men reproachfully assailed; the fear of punishment operating on the agents more immediately concerned, and in fact every consideration, that should influence men, pressed them to a re-deliverance of Morgan to his friends and to society, if it had been possible for them to do so. The people of the western counties, fully aware of the leading circumstances of this transaction, and having had more than two years for inquiry and reflection, have arrived to the decision with unexampled unanimity, that this man has become a victim and a sacrifice.

It is conceded that the facts herein detailed to show the interference of masonry in the administration of justice, come chiefly under the head of circumstantial evidence—of its weight and conclusiveness, the Senate will judge; but it is entirely certain that it fully justifies the opinion of the commissioner, Daniel Mosely, Esq., expressed in a paragraph of his report to the Senate, in which he states that, "as to his fate subsequently thereto, it is not yet developed, nor can it be anticipated with much confidence, to be judicially determined by any tribunal over which men have control."

The committee will now proceed to remark upon other evidence which has come to their knowledge, in reference to the subject before them, of a different but highly alarming character, and calculated more directly to impress upon the Senate the necessity of ulterior legislation. Many masons at the West, whose feelings had been aroused by the enormities of the institution committed in that quarter, learned from witnessing the temper of the people, that they should be protected in any infractions of its laws. They were satisfied beyond controversy that the strange oaths of an institution, governed by iniquitous principles, and used for evil, and sometimes for murderous purposes, ought in no respect to bind the consciences or conduct of those who had imprudently taken them. They saw the absurdity of supposing that any human being could be bound by an oath appealing to the Supreme Being when that very oath enjoined an obligation to do that which is in opposition to the laws of both God and man. They finally assembled at Le Roy in convention, on the 19th of February, 1828, and frankly and truly stated to the world, the substance of the masonic oaths and obligations. One of them is . . . distinguished as No. 1, and is the obligation of the royal arch degree. From an examination of its terms, the Senate will perceive that all masons who have taken it and believe in its binding force, will necessarily and perhaps conscientiously carry on to the witness stand, and into the jury-box and indeed into all the departments of justice, a partiality subversive of every principle of right.

Several of those masons who have seceded from the institution, and certified to the public the oaths and obligations alluded to are personally known to a majority of the committee, and they deem it proper to assure the Senate that they are men of standing in the community, whose characters for veracity are beyond the reach of calumny. Upon this oath, and perhaps one or two more, the committee may cite, no comments will be made, as it is apprehended the simplest form in which the subject can be presented to the mind, will be the most forcible.

In the remarks which his Excellency has been pleased to make, in his message to the legislature, in regard to the abduction of William Morgan, and the excited state of public feeling consequent upon it, the committee have observed, not without sensibility, that just appreciation of the purity and intelligence of the western population of the state, which distinctly commands our acknowledgments. This merited eulogium from so high a source is doubly welcome at a period when the opposers of masonry at the West had been nearly overwhelmed by the torrent of misrepresentation, reproach, and ridicule heaped upon them without measure by the friends of that institution in all parts of the state and country. In this condition, they have sustained themselves, and triumphantly too, by the force of their own moral feeling, and without the ordinary means of defense. The public press, that mighty engine for good or for evil, has been, with a few most honorable exceptions, as silent as the grave. This self proclaimed sentinel of freedom has felt the force of masonic influence, or has been smitten with the rod of its power. His Excellency further observes in that part of the message referred to the committee, and in relation to the public feeling aroused at the West, that "it would not be extraordinary if attempts should be made to pervert this honest indignation of the people to selfish and sinister purposes. But the character of those who really feel what they profess upon this subject, affords the best security that the success of such unworthy schemes cannot be great, or of long duration."

In ascertaining the meaning of this paragraph, the committee have not deemed it proper or expedient to go beyond the plain and obvious import of its terms. Any different sense, arising from a different sort of construction, would be gladly avoided, inasmuch as its adoption by the committee would at once put them in the attitude of entire disagreement with his Excellency, and render it doubtful whether the message in this part of it manifested that high regard for dignity of station which is due from every officer of the government.

Nothing is more proper than that all republican legislation should be characterized by the highest degree of frankness and simplicity; and under the guidance of this spirit, we take the liberty to reassure the Senate, that the committee entirely concur in the opinion expressed by his Excellency, in the paragraph quoted above. The political movements at the West, to which his Excellency no doubt alludes, have been characterized thus far, and we trust they will be hereafter, by a great devotion to principle, and activity and firmness in the pursuit of the objects they have proposed. They have proceeded so immediately from the bosom of the people that the ordinary restraints of parties and their discipline, together with the efforts of those politicians who have heretofore influenced public opinion, have been laid aside and regarded with utter indifference. Satisfied beyond all question that the evils inflicted on the state and country, by secret, self-created societies were a thousand fold greater than any that for many years past had been conjured up by the devices of cunning politicians, the people have sought with wonderful unity of design, of principle, and of effort, to destroy, by the peaceful exercise of their right at the polls, the existence of the masonic, as well as all other secret associations.

The wisest and best men among them, who have neither held or desire office have not been able to discover any *better*, or indeed any *other*, mode of effecting this most interesting object. This peaceful mode of overthrowing an institution of such amazing power, by withholding political support from all its members indiscriminately until they shall sunder their obligations to that institution and to each other, and return with us upon equal footing into the social compact, furnishes, perhaps, one of the highest illustrations of the inherent energy and excellence of our republican form of government that has ever been presented. The Autocrat of all the Russias has exerted the force of his edicts against masonry, but without having been able to extirpate it from his dominions. Its existence is suffered in Great Britain, but a member of the royal family is always at the head of the institution, ready to repress any attempt affecting the government. In France, no lodges are allowed to sit without an agent of the government to watch their proceedings; and in Spain, the meeting of the members of a lodge to admit, and actually admitting a new member, is made felony of death. But in this free country, to effect similar objects, no cruel punishments, no governmental force, no state surveillance is at all necessary. Here, every citizen exercises a portion of the state and national sovereignty, and if this is done with a faithful regard to his own interest and that of his posterity, by withholding that, which no one has a right to demand, the great object will be effected. Legislation therefore, brought to bear immediately and directly upon the existence of the institution, if such could be exerted in conformity with the spirit of the constitution, as expounded by a majority, might, nevertheless, be considered as a measure of doubtful expediency; but that legislative enactments of somewhat different character and more prospective in their operation ought to be adopted, seems evident from the fearful relation in which the masonic institution stands, in reference to the rest of the community.

There are now in this state, as appears by a late, and it is believed accurate, enumeration more than 500 lodges of freemasons, and about one hundred chapters. These lodges and chapters have a probable average of 60 members. The whole number of masons then, cannot be less than 30,000; and these are scattered, in pretty nearly equal portions, throughout the whole population of the state.

The efficiency of such a body, and so located, none will doubt. Controlling as it does common funds, and possessing the advantages of secrecy and activity almost unexampled; using the language of signs, and a character for a written language; its members bound by the most solemn obligations to God and their brethren, they can surmount all difficulties. But the most impressive idea of its powers is to be obtained from one of its votaries, who in a public discourse delivered previous to the abduction of Morgan, declares that masonry "is powerful! It comprises men of rank, wealth, office and talent, in power and out of power; and that almost in every place where power is of any importance; and it comprises, among the other class of the community, to the lowest, in large numbers, and capable of being directed by the efforts of others, so as to have the force of concert through the civilized world! They are distributed too, with the means of knowing each other, and the means of keeping secret, and the means of co-operating, in the desk, in the legislative hall, on the bench, in every gathering of men of business, in every party of pleasure, in every enterprise of government, in every domestic circle, in peace and in war, among its enemies and friends, in one place as well as another. So powerful, indeed, is it at this time, that it fears nothing from violence, either public or private, for it has every means to learn it in season, to counteract, defeat and punish it." These men can effect every thing within the compass of human effort. If the order were to exert itself in aid of charitable objects, not an individual in the state could be either hungry or naked; want would be a stranger in our borders; and vast funds would still remain unexpended. If their zeal and industry were turned to the occult sciences, to which they have professed a devotion, the driest and most abstruse problems of the geometricians, the algebraists and the astronomers would, long before this, have been as familiar to us all as the road to market. But if unmindful of charitable objects, and neglecting the pursuit of the arts and sciences, which they have professed as their leading measures, they should, like the rest of mankind, be tempted by the allurements of power to make an effort to acquire it; all will confess, they must be irresistible, so long as the people remained ignorant of their secret designs. Nothing but a belief or knowledge of those designs, and public opinion brought to bear upon them at the ballot boxes, in countervailing measures, would at all check this otherwise resistless power.

The opposers of masonry at the West, entertain no doubt that this institution was originally intended, and is now kept up, for the sole purpose of securing to its members, unjust advantages over their fellow-citizens, in the various concerns of life, but chiefly with the view of facilitating their acquisition of political power. To change this opinion of our western population is utterly impossible. It is fortified by their own observation. Their masonic neighbors confirm it, by talking with freedom of their principles and practices, until they become as familiar to them, as the highway act, or the act regulating common schools. But if they still doubted, they have only to call to mind that when they undertook the great work of reform, three-fourths of all the offices in the country were filled with members of that institution. The operating causes, in producing the success or defeat of a particular candidate, are not always of easy discovery. But when for a long series of years a large proportion of political and public employment is in the hands of any given order of men, it is natural that suspicions should be entertained, that every thing is not right; and when the disproportion of offices held by the members of that order becomes extravagant and enormous, and continue through a long period of time, notwithstanding the revolutions of political power, then suspicion yields to the moral certainty, that there is a principle of evil in operation of fearful and dangerous import. At the annual election last fall, 270,000 votes were given in this state. If the computation that we have 30,000 masons is correct, they will amount to one-ninth part of our voting population, and are of course entitled, upon the principle of numbers, to one-ninth part of all offices. If it should be granted that the members of the order have double the talent and fitness, in proportion to their numbers, they even then would not be entitled to one-fourth of the power of the state, and yet they have held for years, three-fourths, or very near it. Supposing them to possess on the average no higher qualifications than the rest of the community, which is presumed to be correct, with the exception of that practised talent and facility in business, arising from the actual possession of so great a share of official power, it then becomes a mathematical certainty that if they hold only two-thirds of all places of power and trust in the state, their proportion is precisely six times greater than it ought to be, upon the just principle of equality. The state of things here presented, astonishing, and conclusive, as it may appear to some, is, after all, not surprising when the obligation of the higher order of masons to each other is properly considered and understood. The oath . . . explains the whole matter, and renders the existence of masonic political action not only certain but proves beyond the shadow of a doubt that such action is obligatory on all those masons who give to the oath a binding force.

To all these high charges tending so strongly to inculpate and disgrace the masonic institution, no defense has been offered, at all satisfactory to the understanding. It is true the question is sometimes asked, and with much plausibility, is it possible, if the institution is as corrupt and wicked as has been represented, that distinguished and meritorious men, and many such are admitted to be members, would continue parties to such a nefarious compact? To this it is answered that masonry, in the day of its power, allowed none of its members to recede and express their opinion of its principles and practices, without exposing themselves to punishment more horrid and inhuman than any known to the criminal codes of the civilized world. . . . That there are virtuous and excellent men, who belong to the institution, can be doubted by none of us, who look round upon the circle of our relatives, friends and acquaintances. How this fact is compatible with the opinion we maintain, of the character of the institution, neither time nor the occasion will permit us to explain. But now when masonry totters in doubtful empire; when her countenance is blanched with fear; when the rod of her power is broken, and she no longer dares inflict the punishments of her inhuman code, it is believed those men will feel that they have a duty to perform, of great moment to themselves, to posterity, and their country.

The Clerical Appeal

The Morgan crime and its aftermath supposedly revealed an immoral force at work in America. To Americans of the 1820's, conditioned to expect such forces to be at work in the world, the proper and obvious means to counter it was to awaken American churchmen to the danger. But would the clergy take the lead in such a crusade, especially since many clergymen were Masons? The clerical appeal was composed by a group of prominent laymen representing the major religious denominations in New York. Not only was it important to win the clergy away from the Fraternity but to place them at the head of the crusade. The belief expressed in the appeal that an act must be either consonant with the kingdom of God or of Satan provides a good example of the extreme moral stance that characterized the thinking of many in this era.

At a meeting of different denominations of christians, held at the house of John I. D. Nellis, in Lenox, Madison county, N.Y. on the 13th day of October, 1829, EDWARD LEWIS, Esq., was called to the chair, and NEHEMIAH BATCHELLER, Esq., appointed secretary.

After uniting in solemn prayer to God for a blessing on our feeble efforts to restore peace and prosperity to the church of Christ, which has too long been disturbed by the influence of a secret society, it was

Resolved, That Dr. N. Hall and J. Bruce, Esq., Presbyterians; Deacons B. Jones and R. Randall, Baptists; M. Blakeslee, Esq., and J. W. Hubbard, Episcopalians; and C. Avery and N. Batcheller, Methodists,

"An Appeal to Christian Ministers in Connection with Speculative Free Masonry" (no place of publication cited, 1829). This tract is to be found in the Benno Loewy Collection of the Cornell University Library.

be a committee to draft and report an Appeal to those Ministers of the Gospel who are in connection with the Masonic Fraternity.

The meeting adjourned to the 12th of November, at which time the committee above named reported the following, which was unanimously adopted by the meeting, and ordered to be published, AN APPEAL *from those aggrieved members of Christ's Church who cannot fellowship* SPECULATIVE FREE MASONRY—*To all Ministers of the Gospel, of the different denominations of Christians, who are in connexion with the Masonic Fraternity.*

"Thou shalt in any wise rebuke thy neighbor, and not suffer sin upon him" (MOSES). "Be not partaker of other men's sins" (ST. PAUL).

DEAR AND REVEREND SIRS,

We have been taught by you, both from the pulpit and the press, that the Holy Bible is a divine revelation of the will of God to man, and that it is the only revealed will of God that man ever did or ever will receive while in a state of probation; and also, that it clearly points out the whole duty of man, and is a sufficient rule both for our faith and practice. You further taught us that there are two kingdoms set up in the world, viz. the kingdom of Christ and the kingdom of Satan; and that Christ's kingdom is established on the holy principles of justice, mercy, goodness, light, and truth; and that Satan's kingdom is a kingdom of malice, revenge, falsehood, disorder, and darkness. You also taught us that in the present order of things the interests of these two kingdoms were chiefly promoted through the agency of men; and that every soul of man and every act of men belonged to, and went to the support of one or the other of these two kingdoms.

And now, Rev. Sirs, under a conviction that this doctrine which you have preached to us is fully sustained by the word of God, and in view of a day of final retribution, permit us to ask you a few serious and simple questions.

1st. To which of these two kingdoms does *Speculative Freemasonry* belong? If you say to Christ's kingdom, we ask,

2d. Which of the holy men of old first received it, and which of them was first moved by the Holy Ghost to reduce it into its present organized system?

3d. In which part of the Bible is that system found? For if it belongs to Christ's kingdom, it is in the Bible and is a part of Revelation; and although secret things belong to God, yet revealed things belong to us and our children.

4th. Where do you find a warrant in the Bible that authorizes you, as ambassadors for Christ, to strike hands with the wicked, and enter into a secret combination and league with unbelievers, who, by their wicked works, prove themselves to be enemies of the cross of Christ?

5th. By what authority do you make use of oaths, which are forbidden by the word of God unless required and recognized by the judicial powers which he hath ordained?

6th. What is your authority for giving your life as a pledge that you will keep all the secrets you have sworn to keep, or as a penal forfeiture should you ever reveal them?

7th. Was John the Baptist a Speculative Freemason—and did he masonically prepare the way of the Lord that he might with facility ascend the Masonic Throne, and assume the office of Masonic High Priest? In a word, was Jesus Christ a Speculative Freemason? If he was, masonry is of Him, and belongeth to his kingdom; and when you go after it, you can with great propriety say to every man (provided he hath money and is of a proper age) Follow me as I follow Christ. But to all women (many of whom manifest a desire to follow Christ) you must say, Whither I go you cannot come. And to all young men, under the age of twenty one years, you can say, If God spares your life to a lawful age, you then, on condition that you pay over a specified sum of money to the Order, may follow me as I follow Christ, into the Lodges, Chapters and Encampments of Speculative Freemasonry.

But if it cannot be proved that Jesus Christ, in his manhood, was a Speculative Freemason, and that masonry is identified with his kingdom on the earth, it is much to be feared that you will fall under his displeasure in that day when he will call you to render an account of the manner you have executed your high and responsible office of minister, sent by Him to his fallen and rebellious creature man. Hear him declare before Pilate, "In secret have I said nothing." Is this the language of a mason? Can His ministers, who have sworn allegiance to masonry, make the same solemn appeal in proof of their innocence? In the execution of your office you told us that it was an unalterable decree of your Lord & King, that there should be no articles of peace entered into unless the following particulars on our part were acceded to, viz. a forsaking and repenting of sin, accompanied by an evangelical faith in Christ, and a full surrender of soul and body, for time and eternity, into his hands. But we are told that you have since, in a multitude of cases, entered into an alliance, both offensive and defensive, with men who love and make a lie, and for the due observance of each and every article contained in this treaty, you have bound yourselves by oaths, penalties and imprecations. We also have it from good authority, that the conditions of this treaty are altogether diverse from those you required of us, which renders your conduct highly suspicious, and it is confidently believed that your treaty will never be ratified in the high court of heaven.

But far be it from us to condemn men before they are convicted. You have God's statute book (the Bible) in your hands. To this law and testimony we appeal. If your conduct in the above cases is supported by this law, we respond a hearty Amen. But as you, by profession, are Bible men, and as we have received and supported you as our spiritual teachers, (which we shall continue to do, provided you remove our conscientious scruples in relation to your masonry) we claim it as our right to ask, and think it your duty to answer the above questions with plain historical facts, and positive precepts from the Bible. Spare yourselves the labor of making absolute and unqualified assertions that masonry is "a good institution," or of adducing traditional evidence, far fetched inference, or abstruse metaphysical reasoning. For this kind of evidence cannot be received in support of an institution which occupies a stand so imposing in our moral and religious world as Speculative Freemasonry does.

Another reason why you ought to furnish us and the world with a "Thus saith the Lord" in support of every part of your masonry is, you have done more than any other class of men in rendering the institution popular. Your ministerial character has given it a religious shade, and in it sinners have found a religion without a cross, and it hath pleased them well; and it is a fact that multitudes have and still are resting their eternal all upon it. Another reason why you ought to furnish us with the required evidence is, that the great Head of the Church hath committed to you in trust the ministry of reconciliation, and you are set apart and ordained for the defence of the gospel; and it is no small part of your work to guard the church of Christ from every sly and oblique approach of heresy. But if masonry is not incorporated with christianity, the conclusion is plain, it is a heresy belonging to the kingdom of Satan. Under this view of the subject you have but one alternative, which is to give the above required evidence or remain under the charge of introducing heresy into the church of Christ.

Another part of your work is to investigate all matters of dissention that may unhappily be introduced into the church of Christ. But many of our ministers and members have taken upon them the name and character of Mason, in addition to that of Christian. This has introduced dissentions and a schism into the church, and we think it your duty to see that it is amicably settled and done away.

Another part of your work is to feed the flock of Christ. But they cannot feed on masonry, until they are made to know that it is the bread of life, or sincere milk of the word of God.

Another reason why you should hasten to give the required evidence is, that sinners are stumbling over your double character, and it will be well for you if their blood is not found in your skirts at the last day.

We do not ask you to prove that those outward forms in use by masons, and which in a christian land are copied from christianity, are lawful when lawfully used. But we ask you to prove that the vital spring or soul of masonry, which is an organized secret, bound with oaths and penalties, and sold for money, in a fraudulent speculation on that weak spot in man's fallen nature which leads him to indulge an itching palm to know something his neighbor does not, is or ever was acknowledged by Christ the savior, as a mean by which his cause and kingdom is to be advanced in the world, or by which sinners are brought to the knowledge of the truth.

Now the truth is, that Speculative Freemasonry is either good or bad; it is right or wrong; there is no middle ground in this case, for Christ saith "He that is not for me is against me, and he that gathereth not with me scattereth abroad." But on the supposition that it is right, that it belongeth to the kingdom of Christ, and is a part of the work he requireth you, as his ministers, to perform, how can your conduct in the present excitement be reconciled with your duty? for you have neither supported or renounced masonry, but have stood like men astonished, and looked on while the church has been rent, and that fellowship and good feeling which should always exist among brethren, has in many cases been destroyed, and in others materially injured. Surely the course you have taken is highly reprehensible; for if masonry in fact and in truth belongs to the kingdom of Christ, you, who profess to know and teach the truth as it is in Christ Jesus, could not have been ignorant of it. And admitting that you knew it to be incorporated with the kingdom of Christ, it is reasonable to suppose that your conduct and decision in relation to the subject would have been prompt and unhesitating; that you would not have forsaken the lodges and chapters of masonry on account of a little opposition and disgrace that fell upon it for having executed its righteous laws on an offending brother; and that you, like men set for the defence of the truth, would have rallied round the standard of masonry, grasped your masonic weapons, and worthily executed every forfeited penalty, and thus have secured the secret mysteries and treasures of masonry. You would also have satisfied the church of Christ, over which you, as under shepherds, preside, that you were doing your duty, and nothing but your duty. You would have given evidence that Christ had no allusion to masonry when he said, "There is nothing covered that shall not be revealed, neither hid that shall not be known;" and also that he excepted masonry when he said, "What I tell you in darkness, that speak ye in light; and what ye hear in the ear, that preach ye upon the house tops." This course, on the supposition that masonry belongs to the kingdom of Christ, would have far better comported with the dignity of your calling. But you have fallen in the rear, and left the "handmaid of religion" to the care and support of those men

Whose pride, and sordid lust for gain,
Press reason, judgment, all their better powers,
To serve their lowest passions in the guilty work
Of treasuring up enormous piles of wealth,
Based on the poor man's groan, the widow's tear, and orphan's cry,

in connection with the common liar, swearer, drunkard, and debauched characters, men who carry the mark of the beast on their foreheads, and who disgrace the age in which they live. That such men should with a sparkling zeal take the lead in support of "the handmaid of religion, the simoner of the world, the pillar of morality," is a phenomenon which we call on you to explain.

But on the supposition that masonry does not belong to the kingdom of Christ, it follows on your own decision that it belongs to the kingdom of Satan; for these two kingdoms, on the authority of your own preaching, include every act of man. Here, on the strength of evidence, we might say many things, but we only say that if it belongs to Satan's kingdom, we know not how to avoid the conclusion that it is emphatically a system that God hates and Satan loves. And with the evidence that is now before the public, how is it possible for any man of sober reflection and christian candor to avoid the conclusion that in going after it you have committed a trespass on an enemy's ground, and are supporting the interests of Anti-Christ among men? and in so doing you may rest assured that the people will entertain doubts in relation to your sincerity and uprightness, and while you are warning them to "renounce the hidden things of dishonesty," to "have no fellowship with the unfruitful works of darkness," the retort, "Physician heal thyself" will fly in your face; and the reflection, that as much attention as you have given to masonry, so much you have robbed the church and neglected the work Christ gave you to do, will exclude every better feeling of the human heart.

You see, Rev. gentlemen, on the supposition that masonry belongs to the kingdom of Satan, that in becoming masons your sin is great; and this alone, while unrepented of, will lower down your spirituality and circumscribe your usefulness; and although you may preach with admirable eloquence and system yet it will be but "as sounding brass and a tinkling symbol;" and this effect will remain until the cause is removed; and this will never be removed by a studied silence and secrecy. No, you have been after masonry, and you have sworn to keep masonry secret; but you have not done it. It is out. Yes, death is not more sure than that the secrets of masonry are before the public (except such as have been invented since the present excitement commenced) and with these secrets your masonic conduct is out too; and although you may ardently desire to maintain both your masonic membership and your ministerial influence, yet the people in their majesty have decided otherwise. They say you ought no longer to sustain a double character, but should turn to the right or left, that is, you should prove that Jesus Christ requires, for the advancement of his kingdom, that his ministers should take upon them oaths, penalties and imprecations by which they are in strict concord joined to men who habitually despise the cross of Christ, or relinquish your obligations and connection, from a just persuasion that no man is or ever can be innocently bound by oaths or otherwise to do that which God hath forbidden; and let christianity, with its duties, crosses and immunities, form your future character. This last course we would piously recommend, while we entreat you to follow the noble example of many of your brethren, who, like you, had taken masonry for better or for worse, yet when they found her to be a spiritual harlot fondly offering to dictate and nurse the flock of Christ, they conscientiously divorced her, and are now enjoying the approbating smiles of Christ and his church.

It is expected that while Satan is suffered to go about as a roaring lion, seeking whom he may devour, his servants will fly to the sable shades of secrecy, the better to manage their dark designs of intrigue and mischief. But what have christians and christian ministers to do with such deeds of darkness?

We do not in an absolute sense say that masonry belongs to the kingdom of Satan; but in view of the united testimony of a cloud of witnesses, who in the face of persecution, danger and death, have made a revelation of the secrets of masonry, taken in connection with our own observation, we must acknowledge that it is our candid and sober opinion that it does. The perilous circumstances in which those early seceders were placed in consequence of the disclosures they made, stamps their testimony with indelible marks of truth, and confirms the correctness of our opinion; and we sincerely believe that its latent principles were first introduced into the heart of man by him who led Eve to the interdicted tree; and at the time when she and her deceived husband partook thereof; the effects of which were soon discovered by their attempts at *Secrecy* among the trees of the garden.

That our ministers, whom we love in the Lord, should in a kind of unsettled and wavering manner still cleave to such an institution is a matter of much grief to us. We are also aggrieved at the apparent reluctance you have manifested of entering into a scriptural investigation of the subject. It is not our design in this Appeal unnecessarily to wake up your tender sensibilities; and you may rest assured that we entertain no uncharitable feelings towards you as men and ministers; but against your masonry we protest; and here the matter must rest until you give us the evidence asked for in this appeal, to put away masonry. Do either of these, & a reconciliation is produced, and our aggrievances redressed. Whether the first or second position is pursued is a matter in which we have no interest or choice; but if masonry is right we wish to know it. If it is wrong, you ought to know it. The sentiments of respect we entertain for you would lead us cheerfully to accommodate you by supporting masonry, could we do it with a clear conscience. But if our views are erroneous and masonry is right, the Bible proves it so to be. That the truth on this subject may be satisfactorily ascertained, we invite you to a candid scriptural investigation of the whole matter. Christianity is accessible by every grade, sect and condition of human beings; and in an open, frank and undisguised manner uniformly invites investigation; and it is the glory and boast of our happy land that no moral, religious, scientific or civil institution is by popular consent acknowledged and received until it has passed this ordeal.

We think it unreasonable to sink under our grievances without giving you a specification of the causes. In the performance of this duty we have freely expressed our opinion in relation to masonry as a system, and your conduct as members of that system. We have also noticed the evidence on which our opinion is founded, which evidence we must receive as truth till better evidence proves it false. We know that many who suspend their fate on the fate of masonry, contradict this evidence, but their words appear to be the legitimate language of masonry, spoken through the medium of its interested members, and as such cannot be received as evidence in the case.

We design to exercise all the tenderness and christian forbearance that the nature of the case will admit. It is not our intention to irritate and inflame those festering wounds with which the church has been smitten in consequence of receiving a stranger to her embrace. Neither do we say that we are altogether clear in this matter; for had we as a church extended that watchful care to you which the scriptures incul-cate, we are confident that you never would have been entangled with masonry, nor the church involved in her present difficulties. But the false tongue of masonry beguiled us, and we thought her innocent if not virtuous. We now see our error, and with penitential tears ask God and you to forgive us. We also ask you to expose the fraud by renouncing her. We do not ask you to publish a formal renunciation of masonry, unless you think it your duty to do so. But we ask you, with repentance and humiliation to renounce it before God, and let your influence against it so appear before men that you will not with masonry distract and scatter the church and destroy those sinners whom, thro' the gospel, you are laboring to save.

You plead sacred obligations and charge us with attempting to bind our brother's conscience. We believe the Bible (which is the proper arbiter by which this matter should be decided) stamps your oaths with a moral turpitude, and awards masonry to the kingdom of Satan. If we are not mistaken in this, you are no more bound by your masonic oaths than you would be had you in some unfortunate moment sworn to murder your own families. In this case you would object to the binding nature of your oaths from the fact that they recognized acts which God hath forbidden. This we think is precisely the case with your masonic oaths. If so, our request is so far from binding our brother's conscience, that it only seconds what God commands.

.   .   .

And now, Rev. Sirs, we indulge a hope that you will not receive this appeal as the sentiment of a few disaffected persons but as the sentiment of the church of Christ generally among all christian denominations, and in every place where Speculative Freemasonry has come to the light and when so received, we anticipate that you will pursue one of three courses, that is, you will give us & the world the required evidence in favor of masonry, vindicate your masonic rights and prove your innocence; or you will renounce masonry and come back to the simplicity of the gospel; or, thirdly, you will treat our Appeal with a studied neglect, if not contempt. If this be your course, we have only to say we have lost all confidence in you. But we shall see you again at the judgment seat of Christ.

N. BATCHELLER, Sec'y.   E. LEWIS, Ch'n.

Political Action

By 1828, the essays, tracts, and newspaper accounts declaring the supposed true intent of the Fraternity were legion. But if the Masons were the force of evil, the agent of the devil working to accomplish his ends, they were employing a very practical means—the possession of political power. Almost from the start of the Antimasonic crusade, politics had been involved as Antimasons sought to oust Masons from office and Masons banded together to keep them there. As the Antimasonic excitement grew, it was inevitable that state-wide organizations would be formed. The first delegates to the New York Antimasonic Convention not only made Antimasonry a factor in state politics but by emphasizing the undemocratic actions and objectives of the Fraternity, they tied defense of democratic principles to the crusade for a restoration of moral society. Note especially their call for public opinion to act as the force restoring the purity of political institutions whose leaders—because of Masonic corruption—were unwilling to purify them.

Resolved—That we earnestly recommend to the citizens of the several counties of this State to procure the establishment of Free Presses, whose editors will fearlessly vindicate the rights of its citizens and laws of the land.

Resolved—That a State Convention, to be composed of Delegates from the several counties of the State of New York equal to double the number of their representatives in the Assembly, be called to meet at the village of Utica on the fourth day of August next, to take measures

Proceedings of a Convention of Delegates Opposed to Freemasonry, which met at LeRoy, Genesee Co., N.Y., March 6, 1828 (Rochester, N.Y.: 1828). This tract is to be found in the Benno Loewy Collection of the Cornell University Library.

for the destruction of the Masonic Institution, for sustaining the liberty of the Press, and asserting the supremacy of the laws, for protecting the rights and privileges of the citizens against the vindictive persecutions of members of the Masonic society, and to take into consideration such other business as the said Convention shall deem expedient in furtherance of such objects—and that it be and is hereby recommended to the different counties in this State to send delegates to the same.

Resolved—That a General Central Committee, consisting of five members, be appointed by this Convention; and that it be and is hereby recommended to the different counties to appoint committees of correspondence and report their names to the General Central Committee at Rochester.

Resolved—That the several towns in the county that have not already done so, be requested to appoint town Committees of Correspondence, and forward their names to the Central Corresponding Committee.

Resolved—That it be and is hereby recommended to the several counties to raise funds for defraying the expenses of publishing the proceedings of this Convention, and such other publications as the General Central Committee may think proper to make, and to defray the expenses heretofore incurred by the different Committees in the investigation of the late outrages, and that such funds be transmitted to the General Central Committee.

Resolved—That the proceedings of this Convention be signed by the Chairman and Secretaries—and that 5,000 copies be published in a pamphlet form for distribution, under the direction of the General Central Committee.

Resolved—That SAMUEL WORKS, HARVEY ELY, FREDERICK F. BACKUS, FREDERICK WHITTLESEY, and THURLOW WEED, of the village of Rochester, be appointed a General Central Committee of Correspondence and Publication.

Mr. Davies, from the Committee to whom was referred the subject of the charges made by Masons against the Morgan Committee, made the following Report, which was read and adopted unanimously.

Whereas reports of the most malignant and scandalous nature have been circulated by the Masonic Fraternity, in relation to the members of the several Committees, commonly denominated the Lewiston Committee, charging them with having misrepresented facts in their possession, and with having from sinister views created an unjust excitement:

And whereas this Convention have had adduced to them, the most satisfactory and conclusive evidence that the said committee have fairly and impartially conducted all their enquiries—therefore,

Resolved—That the said Lewiston Committee are entitled to the thanks of this Convention for their patriotic and praiseworthy exertions, in exposing to the world the extensive Masonic Conspiracy formed in this country, which seemed to threaten the civil liberty of this nation, and that they merit, and we trust will receive the countenance and gratitude of every well wisher to the perpetuity of our free institutions.

Resolved—That all the newspapers in the Union, friendly to the cause of civil liberty, be requested to publish these proceedings.

Mr. Love from the Committee to draft a Memorial to the Legislature, on the subject of unlawful oaths, made a report which was read and adopted by the Convention.

Mr. Livingston, from the Committee appointed to draft a Memorial to Congress, reported the same, which was read and adopted.

Bates Cook, Esq. from the Committee appointed for that purpose, reported an Address to the People of the State, which was read and adopted.

ADDRESS TO THE PEOPLE OF
THE STATE OF NEW YORK

Fellow Citizens,

The Institution of Speculative Free Masonry has existed in these United States ever since the formation of our Government. Assuming to be the patron of science, the protector of morality, and the handmaid of religion, it has been suffered to exist without question or suspicion. Its votaries have ever been enthusiastic and extravagant in praise of its character, principles, and tendency. It is, in their own language, a system not only beautiful, but *divine*—whose principles are the purest morality, whose objects are to inculcate universal benevolence and good will among the brethren, and whose operations have been an extended system of holy and healing charity. It is calculated, they say, to enlighten the ignorant, to reform the bad, to protect the weak, and to relieve the necessitous. We have seen many good men, venerable sages, worthy patriots and pious divines belonging to this Institution, and have suffered ourselves to be lulled into security by the impression that such men could not lend their countenance to a society, whose principles were dangerous to society, government, or religion. Their principles have thus been taken upon trust, and the Institution has been suffered to exist in a community prone to suspect that where all is not open, all is not honest. It is, perhaps, a singular fact that in a free government like ours, a government of opinion operating upon a people jealous of their rights, and peculiarly suspicious and jealous of any secret influence and of any thing that could bear the semblance of an insiduous encroachment upon their liberties, such an Institution should have been permitted to grow and increase in strength without subjecting itself to those investigations which the nature and spirit of our government are so well calculated to encourage. Other secret societies have, after a brief existence, been frowned into oblivion as dangerous to a free government. It is owing, doubtless, to the circumstances above set forth, and to the fact that many whom we esteem as our fathers, brothers, and connexions, are members of this Institution, that Speculative Free Masonry has not shared the fate of other secret societies. Some weight too may be attached to the fact that most men of influence and political eminence, those who are wont to take the lead in affairs that concern the government, have themselves been high officials in the Institution, and of course interested in its support. But whatever the cause may have been, it is certain that Free Masonry has been suffered to exist, and to extend itself in this free government, and that without question or enquiry. Addressing itself to the cupidity, the ambition, the vanity, or the curiosity of individuals, it has gone on increasing like the fame of the classic poet, until it has become wide spread in its influence, extended in its operations, and in its multiplied and mystic ramifications it has become interwoven with the very frame and fabric of society, and secretly connected with all our institutions. A cool observer cannot but look back with astonishment and see how secretly and covertly, and at the same time how *rapidly*, it has spread itself through this union, how speciously it has insinuated and connected itself with almost every interest either of a private or public nature. In the foundation of every public building we have beheld the interference of these mystic artisans with their symbolic insignia—in every public procession we have seen their flaunting banners, their muslin robes, and mimic crowns. In the executive of the State we have beheld a man holding the highest office in the Order, bound to his brethren by secret ties of whose nature, strength, and character we knew nothing. We have seen our Legislature controlled by majorities bound to the Fraternity by the same ties. The ermine of justice we have seen worn by men whose brows were decorated with the gilded mitre of the Order in their midnight and secret meetings. We have seen others of this mystic tie empannelled as jurors to hold the balance of justice between a brother and a stranger to the Order, and that brother capable of communicating with such, his judges, by a mystic and symbolic language, unintelligible to his adversary. We cannot now but be astonished that so much should have passed, and that no danger should have been apprehended. Perhaps it may have occasionally occurred to some minds, more than ordinarily watchful, that some designing men may have made use of the Order as a ladder to their ambition; that more than an ordinary share of official patronage was distributed among the brethren; that the even balance of justice may, in some instances, have been made to incline its scale in favor of a brother; that her descending sword may have been averted from the head of a guilty member by the broad shield of the Order. But these suspicions, if any such have been entertained, were partial, and the Institution has felt itself so strong that it has been supposed that it might safely set at defiance every effort to pull it down.

The year 1826, however, introduced a new era in the history of Masonry and of our country. From that year to the present time, enough has transpired to show in a broad and fearful light the danger of secret institutions. That citizen who will close his eyes to this light is criminally negligent to his own rights and the safety of this Government. The Order has been bold enough to assume to itself powers which belong only to the government of the land; and in the exercise of these assumed powers, has violated the liberty of one citizen, and taken the life of another, for an alleged breach of obligations, which our laws do not recognise.

In September, 1826, Capt. William Morgan, a citizen of this State, was seized under feigned process of the law, in the day time, in the village of Batavia, and forcibly carried to Canandaigua in another county. Capt. Morgan was engaged in the publication of a book which purported to reveal the secrets of Free Masonry. This contemplated publication excited the alarm of the Fraternity, and numbers of its members were heard to say that it should be suppressed at all events. It is known that meetings of delegates from the different lodges in the western counties were held to devise means for most effectually preventing the publication. It is known that the matter was a subject of anxious discussion in many and distant lodges. It is known that the zealous members of the Fraternity were angry, excited, and alarmed, and occasionally individuals threw out dark and desperate threats. It is known that an incendiary attempt was made to fire the office of Col. Miller, the publisher of the book. That this attempt was plotted by Masons, and attempted to be carried into execution by Masons. The gang who seized Morgan at Batavia were Masons. They took him to Canandaigua; after a mock trial he was discharged, but was immediately arrested and committed to prison on a stale or fictitious demand. The next night in the absence of the jailor, he was released from prison by the pretended friendship of a false and hollow-hearted brother mason. Upon leaving the prison door he was again seized in the streets of Canandaigua, and notwithstanding his cries of murder, his voice and cries were suppressed, and he was thrust with ruffian violence into a carriage prepared for that purpose. At Batavia he had been torn from his home, from his amiable wife and infant children. At Canandaigua he had been falsely beguiled from the safe custody of the law, and was forcibly carried, by relays of horses, through a thickly populated country in the space of little more than twenty-four hours to the distance of one hundred and fifteen miles, and secured as a prisoner in the magazine of Fort Niagara. This outrage necessarily required many agents; and to the shame of our country enough masons were found, and of these, too, many who were bound by their official oaths to protect the liberty of the citizen, and prevent the violation of the laws, who readily lent their personal assistance and the aid of their carriages and horses in the transportation of this hapless man to the place of his confinement and subsequent death.

This was not their only outrage. About the same time Col. David C. Miller was also seized in Batavia, under like color of legal process, and taken to Le Roy. He was also seized by Masons, and accompanied to Le Roy by a ferocious band of Masons armed with clubs. He was discharged from the process under which he was arrested, and with lawless violence they attempted to seize him again, but to the praise of the citizens of Le Roy, and to some who were members of the Masonic Fraternity, too, be it spoken, he was rescued, and suffered to return to Batavia. The avowed intention of Col. Miller's seizure was to take him where Morgan was—and where that was may be best gathered from the impious declaration of one of the conspirators, James Ganson, for several years a member of our Legislature, that *"he was put where he would stay put, until God should call for him."*

These acts of outrage and violence at length became the subject of enquiry, and excited the honest indignation of a community, always alive to the rights of the citizen and the violation of the laws. Committees of investigation were appointed in the different counties, which were the scenes of this violence, with instructions to do every thing in their power to ferret out this crime, and trace it to the perpetrators. It was, however, perpetrated under the cover of so much secrecy that it was long before even the course which had been taken with Morgan could be traced. Certainly the Committees did not commence their investigations under the impressions that they should find the Fraternity implicated in the transaction. They were slow to believe, as the public have generally and very properly been slow to believe, that a society which embraces among its members so many worthy and pious men, could have ever conived at so foul a crime. It was considered as a blot upon the escutcheon of Masonry, and Masons were publicly called upon to assist in the investigation of this transaction, for the honor of the Order, and to wipe out the stain. The Committees soon discovered, with no little surprise, that they could expect no assistance from members of the Fraternity. On the contrary every obstacle and impediment was thrown in the way. They found the Fraternity in a hostile attitude. They found that they were made the objects of ridicule, threats and detraction—that their motives were impugned and their characters vilified. Defeat, disgrace and ruin were confidently predicted to them; and certainly no means were spared to give to these predictions the character of prophecy. These acts of violence were made a jest of—the excited feeling of the public was ridiculed—their honest indignation was defied. The Courts have been appealed to for justice—but in very few instances has justice been visited upon the heads of the offenders. The masonic oath was soon found to be a shackle upon the officers and ministers of the law—the lips of witnesses were sealed by a mysterious and invisible influence, or opened only in the utterance of falsehoods. Jurors were influenced in their verdicts by an obligation more powerful than their oaths as jurors. Many of the chief offenders fled the country, and the crime yet remains in a great measure unpunished, and the violated laws unavenged. When it was found that the laws were too weak to vindicate their offended majesty, the Committees appealed to the Legislature of this State to institute an enquiry into these outrages. Here, too, it was found that the obligations which bound members to the Fraternity was stronger than their oaths to support the constitution and the laws—and here too they were baffled and left to seek such redress as a few men could obtain against the united influence, wealth, and determined and persevering hostility of a powerful combination.

When it came to be ascertained that great numbers of the Fraternity had been long engaged in devising means for suppressing Morgan's Book—when it became known that the subject was a matter of discussion in many different and distant Lodges—when it was also known that many individuals, all members of the Fraternity, and some high in civil office, were implicated as accomplices in the actual outrages—when the course pursued by members of the Fraternity generally in relation to the investigation was marked, all cool thinking people began to look farther for the origin of the crime, and felt fully justified in identifying the Masonic Institution with these outrages, and holding that responsible for it.

The matter began to assume a new complexion; the dangers of secret societies began to flash upon the minds of the reflecting; here was a bloody text, which afforded matter for fearful comment. The conviction became general, that the safety of Government and Religion, the rights of the citizen, and the impartial administration of justice, required that this institution should be banished from our soil. The freedom and boldness with which the principles and tendency of the Masonic Institution began now to be discussed, encouraged many honest and conscientious members of the Fraternity, who had heretofore been shackled by fear, to renounce their connection with the Society, and to disclose the nature of those secret obligations which bound them together. Taking upon themselves those horrid obligations as they do, ignorant of their nature and import, there rests no obligation upon them, either legal, moral, or honorable, to consider them of any binding force. On the contrary, the duty which they owe to society and their country, as citizens, the duty which they owe to God and his Church, loudly call upon them to divulge the principles of an Institution so hostile to Government and Religion. This class of men are entitled to the gratitude of the public for their disclosures, and have deserved and should receive the countenance and support of every patriotic citizen, to sustain them against every attempt to injure them or defame their characters. These obligations have been published to the world, and furnished further and weighty evidence of the dangers of the Masonic Institution; with the substantial truth of these obligations, and that they are such as are actually taken, we have every reason to be satisfied, and it encourages us in the pledge which we have mutually given to each other and to the world—that we will use our best endeavours to banish this relic of barbarism from our land. It is upon the subject of the dangers of the Masonic Institution, fellow citizens, that we desire to address you; and we are anxious that you should give the subject that consideration which its importance demands. This is not an ordinary topic. *It is not a question whether this or that man shall be President or Governor—it is not a question whether this or that line of measures shall be pursued—but it is a question of immeasurably greater importance—a question whether the rights of the citizen shall be held sacred —whether the laws shall be impartially administered—whether religion shall be duly reverenced.* *

It may be safely said that secret societies, in their best shape, are useless in a free government, calculated to excite jealousies and suspicions in the breasts of the uninitiated, which may lay the foundation of dissentions and ill will. If their objects are honest and praiseworthy, there is no need of secrecy; honesty needs no cloak, and deeds of charity seek not the cover of darkness. Secrecy and concealment ever afford grounds of suspicion. If, however, Masonry is only what it has ever been professed to be, perhaps it might be safely left for the amusement of full grown children; perhaps they might be safely left to the enjoyment of their mock dignities—their muslin robes—their paste board crowns—and their gilded mitres. But when the obligations which bind

* Italics mine—L. R.

them *"to vote for a brother before any other person of equal qualifications"*—to always support his *"military fame and political preferment in opposition to another"*—to aid and assist a brother in difficulty, so far as to extricate him from the same *"whether he be right or wrong"*—to keep his secrets in all cases inviolably, *"murder and treason not excepted,"* and these under no less penalties than a torturing and ignominious death—then it becomes a question of serious import whether such an Institution can be tolerated in our free Government. By the force of these obligations a member can claim the vote of a brother for any elective office, in derogation of that equality guaranteed to us by our Constitution, and the brethren thus elected gradually obtaining the control of the Executive, Legislative and Judicial departments of the Government, can and must dispense their patronage, in strict consonance with the obligations of this mysterious fraternal tie so that soon the Government, in all its branches, must be controlled by the members of the Order. What guarantee is there for the impartial discharge of official duties, when the officer is shackled by such obligations? What hold have we upon the conscience, the integrity or justice of such a man? Is it his oath to support the Constitution of this State and the United States? Is it his oath to faithfully discharge the duties of the office which he fills? He has taken a previous oath of more horrid import and of paramount obligation to which all other oaths, all other ties, all other duties, must yield. He is not a free man. He stands shackled and bound by invisible and mysterious chains. He cannot do his duty to his country if he would—he has a duty to perform to the Fraternity under the severest penalties of Masonic vengeance. What guarantee have we for the impartial administration of justice? A felon communicates the mystic sign to a brother on the grand inquest—the juror's oath to screen no man from fear, favor or affection, must yield to the obligation to extricate a brother *"whether he be right or wrong."* If he escapes not here, there is the same facility of communication with the jurors who are to try him; and strange would it be if some of the brethren, who have found means to insinuate themselves into every station, should not be found upon the panel—and in a panel where one stout and persevering negative prevents his conviction—or the Judge who tries him may receive the *"grand hailing sign,"* and the purity of the ermine may be sullied by the contamination of Masonic iniquity. If all this is not sufficient, the mystic signal may avail with the executive, and the avenging sword of the law may be turned aside from the execution of justice. Where is the security for justice between man and man? Can a Masonic Judge or Masonic Jurors hold the scales even between adverse parties, when one can appeal for assistance thro' the medium of mysterious signals. This is not all. Witnesses who solemnly appeal to God, to tell the truth, the whole truth, and nothing but the truth, in what they shall be called upon to relate, may be bound under obligations more awful, and under penalties more severe, not to disclose the secrets of a brother, No! though it extend to the *murder* of a fellow being, or to *treason* to the State. Is there then, fellow citizens, any safety in trusting those persons who have taken such obligations, and believe in their binding sanction, with any office in our government? Is there any safety in committing our lives, our liberty, our property, or our reputation, to them as judges or jurors? Is any confidence to be placed in witnesses who have bound themselves under such awful obligations, to keep the secrets of a brother? These obligations strike at the very existence of our Government—at the very foundation of our rights—and at the impartial administration of our laws.

This Institution threatens not only danger to government and the cause of justice, but strikes at the basis of all morality and religion. The obligation not to disclose the secrets of a brother, even in cases of murder and treason, has a tendency to invite the confidence of a brother Mason. Under the sanction of this oath a bold bad man will not fear to disclose the history of his crimes to the ears of the virtuous, to the ears of even a minister of the holy gospel and, secure against detection, make an impudent boast of his iniquities. This will make virtuous men familiar with the detail of crimes and confidants in criminal secrets; and vice is of a character so contagious that one cannot even listen to its history or be familiar with its secrets without some danger of contamination, and that nice, delicate, moral sense which characterizes a virtuous man, must be gradually effaced, and his principles of virtue must be, in a great measure, rendered unsettled. Is Free Masonry the handmaid of religion? that Institution in whose rites and ceremonies the most touching portions of that holy book, which holds out to us the promise of eternal life, are introduced in solemn mockery and represented in the shape of a miserable theatrical farce? where a weak sinful mortal undertakes to personify the Almighty God? where the name of our blessed Saviour and the Holy Trinity are introduced in a vain and

irreverent manner? where the belief of the immortality of the soul is
pledged in a libation from the skull of a masonic traitor? where the life
eternal in the heavens is represented only as one great Lodge, and the
Almighty is blasphemously typified as Grand Master thereof? Is such
an institution the handmaid of Religion? We think we are safe in saying
that the frequent use of profane oaths, the irreverent familiarity with
religious forms and sacred things, the blasphemous mockery of the name
of the Triune God, in the recesses of the lodge-room, are more dangerous to the cause of the benign Religion of Jesus than open and
avowed infidelity. It is to be feared that many substitute and rely upon
the religion of Masonry instead of the religion of Him who died to
atone for our sins, or if not, they come to the belief that all religion is
only the farce which their impious ceremonies represent it to be. It is
time those delusions were dispelled. Masonry now stands before us in
its naked deformity, stripped of its tinsel ornaments and solemn mum-
mery. It behooves us to take warning from the past and receive instruction from the school of experience. We see in these disclosures the
same principles which deluged France in blood and were the cause of
the dark crimes which stained that distracted country during the period
of her sanguinary Revolution. We see the same principles which governed Illuminism in the last century and lighted her path in that foul
plot which would have substituted anarchy for government and civil
rule, and Atheism for the Religion of the Cross. It is from the bosom of
Free Masonry that this dark conspiracy originated. To the bosom of
Free Masonry every revolution and conspiracy, which has agitated
Europe for the last fifty years, may be distinctly traced, and the secret
workings of this all pervading order can be clearly seen. The governments of the world are beginning to be awake to the danger. Russia has
suppressed the Order in her own dominions; Spain has suppressed it,
and our sister Republic of Mexico is exerting herself to crush one of
its hydra heads. Shall we alone look tamely on, and use no endeavors
to check the spread of its contaminating principles? You ask how it is
to be suppressed in this free Government. They confidently boast that
it is not in the power of man to suppress it—that even this *Government
itself* with all its power cannot do it. This may be true. But there is a
power in this free land superior even to our Government, and which
guides, controls and directs it, and that power is *public opinion.* The
laws we have found too weak; *Government may be too weak; but there*

is a moral force in public opinion, *which must, in this free country, crush every thing, however powerful, which is arrayed against it—this opinion speaks in our public meetings—it speaks from the sacred desk —it speaks through the organ of the press—it speaks through the ballot boxes,** when masons appeal to you in this manner for support and countenance. This power, fellow citizens, you have under your control. It is the only legitimate and proper force that can be put in operation in this emergency, and in this country. This is a power for you to wield —and in its exercise remember the warning voice of the Father of his country, to *"beware of all secret societies."*

As the Convention was about to adjourn, Mr. Thompson offered the following resolution, which was unanimously adopted:

Resolved, That the thanks of this Convention be presented to our highly respected fellow citizen, Gen. William Wadsworth, the President of this Convention, for his patriotic and able discharge of the duties of the Chair, and also to Doct. Brown and Col. Fleming, as Secretaries on this interesting occasion.

WILLIAM WADSWORTH, President

MATHEW BROWN, } Secretaries
ROBERT FLEMING, }

ANTI-MASONIC DECLARATION OF INDEPENDENCE

At an adjourned meeting of the Convention of Seceding Masons held at Le Roy, July 4th, 1828, SOLOMON SOUTHWICK, *President,* and REV. DAVID BERNARD, *Clerk.*

AUGUSTUS P. HASCALL, Chairman of the Committee appointed to draft a DECLARATION OF INDEPENDENCE, from the Masonic Institution, reported the following, which was accepted and signed.

When men attempt to dissolve a system which has influenced and governed a part of community, and by its pretensions to antiquity, usefulness and virtue, would demand the respect of all, it is proper to submit to the consideration of a candid and impartial world the causes which impel them to such a course. We, seceders from the masonic institution, availing ourselves of our natural and unalienable rights,

---

* Italics mine—L. R.

and the privileges guaranteed to us by our constitution, freely to discuss the principles of our government and laws, and to expose whatever may endanger the one, or impede the due administration of the other, do offer the following reasons for endeavouring to abolish the order of Freemasonry, and destroy its influence in our government.

In all arbitrary governments free inquiry has been restricted as fatal to the principles upon which they were based. In all ages of the world tyrants have found it necessary to shackle the minds of their subjects to enable them to control their actions; for experience ever taught that the free mind exerts a moral power that resists all attempts to enslave it. However forms of governments heretofore have varied, the right to act and speak without a controlling power, has never been permitted. Our ancestors, who imbibed principles of civil and religious liberty, fled to America to escape persecution; and when Britain attempted to encroach upon the free exercise of those principles, our fathers hesitated not to dissolve their oaths of allegiance to the mother country, and declare themselves free and independent, and exulting millions of freemen yet bless their memories for the deed. A new theory of government was reduced to practice in the formation of the American republic. It involved in its structure principles of equal rights and privileges, and was based upon the eternal foundation of public good. It protects the weak and restrains the powerful, and extends its honors and emoluments to the meritorious of every condition. It should have been the pride of every citizen to preserve this noble structure in all its beautiful symmetry and proportions. But the principle of self aggrandizement, the desire to control the destinies of others and luxuriate on their spoil, unhappily still inhabits the human breast. Many attempts have already been made to impair the freedom of our institutions and to subvert our government. But they have been met by the irresistible power of public opinion and indignation, and crushed. In the mean time the masonic society has been silently growing among us, whose principles and operations are calculated to subvert and destroy the great and important principles of the commonwealth. Before and during the revolutionary struggle, masonry was but little known and practiced in this country. It was lost amid the changes and confusion of the conflicting nations and was reserved for a time of profound peace to wind and insinuate itself into every department of government, and influence the result of almost every proceeding. Like many other attempts to overturn governments and destroy the liberties of the people, it has chosen a time when the suspicions of men were asleep, and with a noiseless tread, in the darkness and silence of the night, has increased its strength and extended its power. Not yet content with its original powers and influence, it has of late received the aid of foreign and more arbitrary systems. With this accumulation of strength it arrived at that formidable crisis when it bid open defiance to the laws of our country in the abduction and murder of an inoffending citizen of this republic. So wicked was this transaction, so extensive its preparation, and so openly justified, that it roused the energies of an insulted people, whose exertions have opened the hidden recesses of this abode of darkness and mystery, and mankind may now view its power, its wickedness and folly.

That it is opposed to the genius and design of this government, the spirit and precepts of our holy religion, and the welfare of society, generally, will appear from the following considerations.

It exercises jurisdiction over the persons and lives of citizens of the republic.

It arrogates to itself the right of punishing its members for offences unknown to the laws of this or any other nation.

It requires the concealment of crime and protects the guilty from punishment.

It encourages the commission of crime by affording the guilty facilities of escape.

It affords opportunities for the corrupt and designing to form plans against the government and the lives and characters of individuals.

It assumes titles and dignities incompatible with a republican government, and enjoins an obedience to them derogatory to republican principles.

It destroys all principles of equality by bestowing its favors on its own members, to the exclusion of others equally meritorious and deserving.

It creates odious aristocracies by its obligations to support the interest of its members in preference to others of equal qualifications.

It blasphemes the name and attempts the personification of the Great Jehovah.

It prostitutes the sacred scriptures to unholy purposes to subserve its own secular and trifling concerns.

It weakens the sanctions of morality and religion by the multiplication of profane oaths and immoral familiarity with religious forms and ceremonies.

It discovers in its ceremonies an unholy commingling of divine truth with impious human inventions.

It destroys a veneration for religion and religious ordinances, by the profane use of religious forms.

It substitutes the self righteousness and ceremonies of masonry for vital religion and the ordinances of the gospel.

It promotes habits of idleness and intemperance, by its members neglecting their business to attend its meetings and drink its libations.

It accumulates funds at the expense of indigent persons, and to the distress of their families, too often to be dissipated in rioting and pleasure, and in its senseless ceremonies and exhibitions.

It contracts the sympathies of the human heart for all the unfortunate, by confining its charities to its own members; and promotes the interest of the few at the expense of the many.

An institution, fraught with so many and great evils, is dangerous to our government, and the safety of our citizens, and is unfit to exist among a free people. We, therefore, believing it the duty we owe to God, our country and posterity, resolve to expose its mystery, wickedness, and tendency, to public view, and we exhort all citizens who have a love of country and a veneration for its laws, a spirit of our holy religion and a regard for the welfare of mankind, to aid us in the cause which we have espoused—and appealing to Almighty God for the rectitude of our motives we solemnly absolve ourselves from all allegiance to the masonic institution and declare ourselves free and independent. And in support of these resolutions, our government and laws, and the safety of individuals against the usurpations of all secret societies, and open force, and against the "vengeance" of the masonic institution, "with a firm reliance on the protection of Divine providence, we mutually pledge to each other, our lives, our fortunes, and our sacred honor."

July 4, 1828

The Crusade and the Party

Thurlow Weed

> In the following autobiographical piece by Thurlow Weed we gain
> a sense of the difficulties and the contradictions that plagued a
> party built on a crusade. Do you choose candidates on the basis of
> their Antimasonic zeal or on their general qualifications and popular
> appeal? Do you support national candidates who may be indifferent
> to the crusade? In the atmosphere of political maneuvering the cru-
> sade might serve as a source of embarrassment and a hindrance to
> effective action. Antimasonry provided Weed with a start in politics,
> but it is not surprising that ultimately he and others in the party
> sought to escape its restrictions.

I will now, as briefly as the nature and importance of the question
will permit, give a history of political Anti-Masonry. As the town
meetings in the spring of 1827 were approaching, the citizens of several towns in the county of Genesee, and of one town in the county of
Monroe, of their own volition refused to vote for Masons as supervisors
or justices of the peace. That circumstance occasioned a good deal of
conversation and solicitude among the prominent citizens of Rochester,
Canandaigua, Auburn, Genesee, Batavia, Lewiston, and Buffalo, who
had been actively engaged in the investigations concerning the abduction, the imprisonment, and probable murder of Morgan, and who yet
had not contemplated political action, and who were unwilling to allow
the question to assume such aspects. As soon, therefore, as it was found
practicable, there was a consultation between Francis Granger, William
H. Seward, James Wadsworth, Samuel Works, Harvey Ely, Frederick
F. Backus, Frederick Whittlesey, Thurlow Weed, Trumbull Cary, David

Harriet Weed, ed., *Life of Thurlow Weed* (Boston, 1884), I, 229–325.

E. Evans, Bates Cook, George H. Boughton, Albert H. Tracy, Thomas C. Love, and George F. Talbot. Messrs. Ely, Backus, and Love were at first inclined to favor political action, but after free and frank discussion they acquiesced in the views entertained by all the other gentlemen present, and it was therefore determined to repress, as far as we were able, the disposition to carry the question into politics. The pressure for political action was most earnest from seceding Masons, a large class of influential men, who insisted that the ballot was the only weapon that could be successfully wielded against the fraternity, and who insisted that by no other means, and in no other way, could they be protected from the "vengeance" of the institution which they had renounced. We were unable, however, as the town meetings approached, in the spring of 1827, to restrain the citizens of Le Roy, Stafford, Elba, etc., in Genesee County, and of Wheatland, in Monroe County, where tickets, from which Masons were excluded, ran and were elected. Rochester had already become the centre of Anti-Masonry. From that point the movements, whether of a judicial or legislative character, emanated.

We continued, in our conversations and correspondence, to repress political agitation, until an incident occurred which changed our views and policy. From the incorporation of Rochester as a village down to the summer of 1827, Dr. Frederick F. Backus had been its treasurer, elected year after year without opposition. Dr. Backus having been attending a patient until a late hour in the night of the 12th day of September, 1826, observed a carriage standing in the street surrounded by several persons, who started off in one direction, while the carriage moved off in another as he approached it. Subsequently, he saw those persons emerge from their hiding-places and go in the direction the carriage had taken. After it became known that Morgan had been taken from the Canandaigua jail in a carriage, which was driven away in the direction of Rochester, Dr. Backus, by comparing dates, became satisfied that Morgan was a prisoner in the carriage whose mysterious movements he had observed, and from that hour he took an active part in the investigation, and became a zealous opponent of Masonry. When the village election approached, Dr. Backus, as usual, was placed in nomination. No person was nominated as an opposing candidate, nor was it known at the polls that any other person was being voted for for treasurer. But upon a canvass of the votes, it appeared that Dr. John B.

Elwood was elected treasurer. This *coup d'état,* so secretly and success-fully accomplished, awakened immediate and wild excitement through-out the village. It was like a spark of fire dropped upon combustible materials. "The blow was struck but the hand concealed," according, as it was alleged, to the obligations of the Order. Dr. Elwood, like Dr. Backus, was much respected, belonged to the same political party, and was not a Freemason; but his election, unknown even to himself until after the votes were canvassed, was attributed to the secret mandate of the village lodge; nor in their exultations over the result did the Masons deny that "impeachment."

Our petitions for a law changing the mode of selecting grand juries having been denied by the legislature of 1827, while the portals of justice were closed against us, we now decided to appeal through the ballot-boxes to the people. Early in September of 1827 a Monroe County Convention of Anti-Masons was called for the purpose of nom-inating members of Assembly. Public sentiment was then divided be-tween the friends and opponents of the administration of John Quincy Adams. As all the members of the Morgan Committee (Messrs. Works, Ely, Backus, Whittlesey, and Weed), with the exception of Mr. Whit-tlesey, were supporters of the administration, the Masons, irrespective of party, became identified with the Democratic, or, as it was then called, the "Jackson party." We took the field a month earlier than it was usual to make nominations. While the Anti-Masonic sentiment was strong among the farmers, it was weak in the villages, especially among the wealthy and influential classes. It was difficult, therefore, to find in the village of Rochester a well-known and prominent citizen who would take an anti-Masonic nomination. An intimate friend (Tim-othy Childs), who was exceedingly anxious to obtain a seat in the legislature, and to whom the nomination was offered, found it difficult to restrain his indignation at the idea of becoming the candidate of a "contemptible faction." I left him, after an excited interview, with the assurance that he would have to take the responsibility of accepting or declining our nomination. After his nomination, we had another stormy interview; but as Messrs. Works, J. K. Livingston, Dr. Backus, and myself were his best friends, he quietly but sulkily acquiesced, re-garding it, however, as fatal to all his political hopes. Two or three weeks afterwards, as the Jackson County convention was about to meet,

Addison Gardiner, a Jackson man, who had the sense to discern and comprehend the significance of Anti-Masonry, endeavored to break our line by offering Mr. Childs *their* nomination for the Assembly. The Jackson men did not require Mr. Childs either to *accept* their nomination or to *decline* the Anti-Masonic one, thus making him a sort of political equestrian, riding two horses. So far, all was smooth; but when Mr. Childs reported the arrangement to our committee, he was kindly but peremtorily informed that he must immediately accept or decline our nomination. This put him in a "tight place." But in reflecting upon the fact that we were his best and only real friends, he despondingly accepted our nomination, and during the same evening he was further discomfited by hearing persons offer bets freely that the Anti-Masonic ticket would not poll five hundred votes in the county. But the result showed how little the most intelligent and influential villagers knew of the spirit abroad among the farmers. The Anti-Masonic candidates were elected by a majority of 1700. Although not nominated as such, Francis Granger and Robert C. Nicholas, of Ontario, Nathan Mixer, of Chautauqua, and Morris F. Sheppard, of Yates, acted and became identified with the Monroe County Anti-Masons.

The following year, Mr. Childs, who became an Anti-Mason so grudgingly, was elected to Congress, where he served as an Anti-Mason four years.

State and presidential elections were now approaching. The Anti-Masonic element had developed sufficient political strength to attract the attention of parties and politicians. The Masons generally, without reference to their political antecedents, sought refuge in the Jackson or Democratic party. Most of the Anti-Masonic leaders had been Clintonians and were supporters of Mr. Adams' administration. President Adams, immediately after the abduction of Morgan was proven, wrote a letter saying that he was not, never had been, and never should be a Mason. General Jackson was known to be an adhering Mason. Hence the Anti-Masons of Western New York, though previously about equally divided in political sentiment, became early open and zealous supporters of Mr. Adams for President. The feeling of Masons, exasperated by the existence of a political organization which made war upon the institution of Freemasonry, became intensely so by the renunciation of Masonry by ministers, elders, and deacons of the Presbyterian, Methodist, and Baptist churches. The conflict therefore became more embittered and relentless, personally, politically, socially, and ecclesiastically, than any other I have ever participated in, and more so, probably, than any ever known in our country. Thousands of Masons, innocent of any wrong, and intending to remain neutral, were drawn into the conflict, when all were denounced who adhered to the institution. On the other hand, the Anti-Masons maintained that the abduction and murder of Morgan resulted legitimately from the obligations and teachings of the Order.

Meantime, the State election was approaching; and as the Anti-Masons had extended their political organization not only throughout all the western counties, but as it was attracting the attention of many citizens in other sections, it became the occasion of annoyance to both of the great political parties of the State. The Democrats saw in it an element which, if won over to the Adams party, would constitute a majority; and while most of the Adams politicians were anxious to conciliate the Anti-Masons, the few adhering Masons belonging to that party indignantly repudiated any such alliance. Masonry, as I have before remarked, having sought and found protection in the Jackson party, Anti-Masons naturally affiliated with the Adams party. Having been in 1824 a zealous supporter of Mr. Adams for President, I enjoyed in an equal degree the confidence of the Adams men and the Anti-Masons. The policy of nominating candidates for governor and lieutenant-governor by the National Republican (Adams) Convention for whom the Anti-Masons could consistently vote, was transparent. Indeed, it was scarcely denied that if the National Republican and Anti-Masonic vote could be united, the Jackson party would lose the State. Francis Granger, of Ontario, a prominent National Republican, and a warm supporter of Mr. Adams before and after his election, although he took part in the investigation which sought a vindication of the laws against those who were connected with the conspiracy to abduct Morgan, was not as yet a political Anti-Mason. He was well-known and popular. I spent several weeks in visiting influential National Republicans in different parts of the State with the hope of inducing them to nominate Mr. Granger for governor. And when the convention met at Utica that result was confidently anticipated. Delegates from the rural districts generally were for Mr. Granger, while those from the River Counties, Long Island, and the city of New York were warmly in favor of Smith Thompson, a judge of the Supreme Court of the United States, of conceded ability and irreproachable character. The canvas, though animated, was conducted in a good spirit. All were anxious for success, but all could not see and think alike. We assured the convention that while two thirds or three fourths of our friends would vote for Judge Thompson, the extreme or ultra Anti-Masons would nominate an independent ticket, for which votes enough would be cast to secure the election of the Jackson candidates. On the other hand, it was maintained by influential delegates that the nomination of Mr. Granger avowedly to secure the Anti-Masonic vote would offend so many National Republicans as to jeopardize not only the State, but the electoral ticket; and this view of the question, accepted by a majority of the delegates, finally led to the nomination, by a close vote, of Smith Thompson for governor. Mr. Granger was then nominated by acclamation as a candidate for lieutenant-governor.

I left the convention as soon as I discovered that the nomination of Judge Thompson was inevitable, in the hope of rendering it acceptable to my Anti-Masonic friends. Two days' observation and experience, however, satisfied me that this was hopeless. An Anti-Masonic paper at Canandaigua, edited by W. W. Phelps (who subsequently became a Mormon, and is now, I understand, one of Brigham Young's elders), denounced that nomination, and came out with a call for an Anti-Masonic State convention. The Anti-Masonic paper at Le Roy responded warmly. In consultation with a few discreet friends, it was deemed advisable that Judge Thompson should be informed of the state of feeling in the West; and the day after my return to Rochester, I hastened eastward on this errand. A committee, consisting of John A. King, of Queens, George Tibbitts, of Rensselaer, and Henry W. Delavan, of Albany, was appointed to wait on Judge Thompson and inform him of his nomination. The judge was understood to be at Saratoga, and after the adjournment of the convention, the committee left for Saratoga; but on their arrival they learned that he had just left for Poughkeepsie. Being at Saratoga, they remained for twenty-four hours, so that when I reached Albany I ascertained that the committee had taken the morning boat for Poughkeepsie. Leaving Albany in the

afternoon boat, I encountered the committee as I landed at Poughkeepsie, waiting to take the same boat for New York. Informing them that
I had important information to impart to them, they returned with me
to the hotel, where I apprised them of the real condition of things in
the western counties, and of the nature of my mission. They replied
that even if it were desirable that Judge Thompson should decline the
nomination, it was too late, for they had obtained his reluctant acceptance within the last hour. They consented, however, at that late and
unpropitious time, to accompany me to his residence, where I discharged an embarrassing duty. Judge Thompson was equally embar-
rassed and annoyed, all the more annoyed from the circumstance that
he had not desired the nomination, and after several hours' consideration had given the committee his reluctant consent to accept it. I expressed the opinion that votes enough would be thrown away upon Mr.
Southwick (whom I saw in Albany, and who was more than ready to
take an Anti-Masonic nomination) to defeat his election. Mr. King
concurred with me in opinion. Mr. Tibbitts thought that, although it
might have been wise to have nominated Mr. Granger for governor, yet
the declension of Judge Thompson under the circumstances that existed would render the success of any ticket impossible. Mr. Delavan,
exasperated by what he regarded as factious opposition, strongly deprecated the idea of Judge Thompson's withdrawal. The judge, therefore, a good deal disturbed by the interview, declined to withdraw his
acceptance, and between twelve and one o'clock we returned to the
hotel, resolved thenceforward to do our duty and hope for the best.

An Anti-Masonic State convention was immediately called, which
met at Utica, and nominated Francis Granger, of Ontario, for governor,
and John Crary, of Washington County, for lieutenant-governor. This
placed Mr. Granger in a position of peculiar embarrassment. He had
not desired, and much less had he solicited, any nomination, and yet
he stood complicated by conflicting nominations from conventions with
the principles of both of which he sympathized. It was difficult in
accepting either or in declining either of these nominations to avoid
offense, and yet this awkward responsibility was the result of circumstances entirely beyond control. Both nominations had been accorded
to him in good faith by his personal and political friends. After mature
deliberation he decided to decline the Anti-Masonic nomination for
governor, and to accept the National Republican nomination for lieu-

tenant-governor. His letter on that occasion, extricating himself from the false position which arbitrary circumstances placed him in, was so direct, frank, and manly as to command very general approval. The anti-Masons then nominated Solomon Southwick for governor in his stead. The election was very warmly contested. My own position was almost, if not quite, as embarrassing as that of Mr. Granger. I could not, consistently with my sense of what was due to other principles involving the welfare of the country, support the Anti-Masonic State ticket, although I knew that it would be voted for by one half or two thirds of my Anti-Masonic friends. The course which I deemed it proper to take in reference to the nomination of Southwick was briefly indicated in the following editorial in the *Anti-Masonic Enquirer,* of Tuesday, September 23, 1828.

> We publish to-day the proceedings of a meeting said to have been numerously attended at the capitol, in the city of Albany, where Solomon Southwick was nominated for governor of this State. This nomination, emanating from that at Le Roy, has been approved cordially, we believe, by the Ontario and reluctantly by the Wayne County Convention. Other counties, in town and county meetings, will indicate their approbation of this measure, and Mr. Southwick will receive the divided support of the Anti-Masonic party.
>
> This unwelcome state of things has been brought upon us by the cunning of Freemasonry. It is a crisis full of perplexing interest. Both political parties have contributed their exertions to cripple and embarrass the cause of the people. They have juggled us out of a candidate for governor. But a determination to adhere to the principles they profess now drives a large number of our friends into a measure of at least doubtful expediency.
>
> The strongest suggestions of patriotism and the highest considerations of duty united to interest the prominent men of the State against an institution towards which Washington pointed his warning admonitions. But these high inducements failed to influence distinguished partisans. The violated laws of the country and the unavenged blood of a murdered citizen were not questions of sufficient importance to withdraw them from the pursuit of political honors. The road to office, obstructed by the power and influence of Masonry, did not appear direct enough to appease their hopes. The people were left to oppose Freemasonry without the

aid of the laws and unsupported by the countenance of leading
men. Indeed, so cautious were the prominent politicians, that none
of them could be induced to identify their efforts and commit their
political fortunes to the hands of men devoted to the cause of civil
liberty. Political astrologers could not clearly discern the star by
which they were to be conducted to the object of their ambition,
and therefore refused to espouse the cause of truth and justice.
Hence the embarrassments by which we are surrounded.

If under these multiplied difficulties the Anti-Masons incline
to bestow their votes upon Mr. Southwick, though our conviction
of duty will compel us to withhold our own from him, we shall by
no means impugn their motives. The people are entitled to a candidate. Those Anti-Masons who believe Mr. Southwick a suitable
person for governor act consistently and honorably in supporting
him. We, too, shall vote for an Anti-Mason, according to the
"strictest order of the sect." But we ask of our friends the same
privilege which we accord to them—the right of exercising the
elective franchise independently.

The election resulted in a vote of 136,785 votes for Van Buren,
106,415 for Thompson, and 33,335 for Southwick. So that while Mr.
Van Buren was chosen, the combined vote of Thompson and Southwick left him in a minority of more than 3,000. It is possible, though
not probable, that Mr. Granger's nomination by the Republican convention, supported as he would have been by the Anti-Masons, might
have then overthrown the Albany Regency. As it was, Mr. Van Buren's
election enabled his party to hold the State for the twelve succeeding
years.

•   •   •

The election of 1828 imparted increased confidence, vigor, and
strength to the Anti-Masonic party. It not only established itself firmly
in the counties west of Cayuga Bridge, but made an important lodgment
in Washington and Cortland, and revolutionized isolated towns in
Madison, Onondaga, Oswego, Jefferson, Chenango, and Delaware.
Wm. H. Maynard, Hiram F. Mather, George H. Boughton, Timothy
H. Porter, and Moses Hayden of the Senate were political Anti-Masons.
Abner Hazeltine and Nathan Mixer, of Chautauqua; David Burt and
Millard Fillmore, of Erie; Calvin P. Bailey and John Haskell, of Gen-

esee; Philo C. Fuller and Titus Goodman, of Livingston; John Garbutt, Heman Norton, and Reuben Willey, of Monroe; John Guernsey, of Niagara; John Dickson, Walter Hubbell, and Robert C. Nicholas, of Ontario; George W. Flemming, of Orleans; and Morris F. Sheppard, of Penn Yan, all Anti-Masons, were elected to the Assembly. The practical effect of this partial triumph was the enactment of a law taking from the sheriffs of counties the selection of grand jurors.

Meanwhile my paper, the *Anti-Masonic Enquirer*, with a circulation in what was known as the "infected district" quite unparalleled, had extended not only to the middle and northern counties of New York, but was being freely ordered from the Western Reserve in Ohio, from Alleghany, Somerset, Union, Lancaster, and Chester counties in Pennsylvania, and from all parts of Vermont.

The cause was being aided simultaneously by the letters of renouncing Masons, some of which, like that from Cadwallader D. Colden, a distinguished lawyer and politician of the city of New York, were very effective. The renunciation of Elder Barnard, a talented and popular Baptist minister in Chautauqua County, was soon followed with a book from that divine, revealing the secrets of the Royal Arch Degree of Masonry. A convention of seceding Masons, formidable in numbers and ability, met at Le Roy, by whom the truth of the revelations made by William Morgan and Elder Barnard were solemnly affirmed. Large editions of the proceedings of that convention were printed and circulated in New York, Ohio, Pennsylvania, Vermont, Connecticut, and Massachusetts, adding fuel to the flames previously kindled. The *Anti-Masonic Review*, under the auspices and management of Henry Dana Ward, a renouncing "Three Degree Mason," was about this time established in the city of New York. Mr. Ward was a gentleman of education, refinement, and ability. His character was unblemished. He was impressive and earnest. His writings carried conviction with them. His *Review* became popular, and while the excitement lasted was very influential.

The two individuals, among those prominently connected with the Morgan investigation, who most reluctantly yielded to the influences which carried the question into politics were Frederick Whittlesey and myself. Mr. Whittlesey was the proprietor and editor of the Rochester *Republican*, a Democratic journal. He was efficient and influential, stood well with his party, and might look forward to the gratification of a reasonable ambition. Appointed by a committee of his fellow-citizens to investigate the violation of the laws, he discharged that duty fearlessly, but he had not contemplated the possibility of becoming alienated from his party. I, in like manner, held a responsible position in the administration party, as I had enjoyed until that period the confidence of Governor Clinton, who had himself relieved me and many other old friends by taking ground for Jackson, while Mr. Adams had made the path of duty smooth by becoming an Anti-Mason.

.   .   .

The election of 1833 demonstrated unmistakably not only that opposition to Masonry as a party in a political aspect had lost its hold upon the public mind, but that its leading object, namely, to awaken and perpetuate a public sentiment against secret societies, had signally failed. The Jackson party was now more powerful than ever in three fourths of the States in the Union. The National Republican party was quite as fatally demoralized as that to which I belonged. This discouraging condition of political affairs, after a consultation with W. H. Seward, Francis Granger, Trumbull Cary, Bates Cook, Millard Fillmore, Frederick Whittlesey, John C. Spencer, Philo C. Fuller, Edward Dodd, George W. Patterson, Timothy Childs, Lewis Benedict, John Townsend, Thomas Clowes, Nicholas Devereux, James Wadsworth, Thomas C. Love, and others, resulted in a virtual dissolution of the Anti-Masonic party. All or nearly all of our leading friends having no affinities of sentiment or sympathy with the Jackson party found themselves at liberty to retire from political action, or unite with the then largely disorganized elements of opposition to the national and State administrations. I had by this time become irreconcilably opposed to the Regency, and fell naturally into association with their opponents. The *Evening Journal* went diligently and zealously to work organizing the elements of opposition throughout the State into what soon became the "Whig" party.

Seward Stands by the Crusade

William H. Seward

> Despite its shortcomings the Antimasonic crusade provided those politicians who espoused the cause with an issue. If they could convince the voters that one's stand on the Masonry question transcended all other positions, they could expect to gain power. By 1831, it must have been evident that this simple black or white view of politics had been rejected; indeed, the Antimasons themselves introduced other issues into their campaigns. However, William Seward and other Antimasonic leaders were apparently still convinced that they must simplify politics and present the voter with a choice of pro or antimasonry. Seward, as leader of the Antimasonic minority in the New York State legislature, described the political situation in those terms. A year later the Antimasonic party was dead and this crusade in politics ended.

We regret to state that the act by which the government of the state assumed upon itself the prosecution of the murderers and kidnappers of William Morgan has been suffered to expire; and that those prosecutions are to be in effect abandoned, although several indictments against the worst offenders, remain to be tried. It seems not to be deemed necessary any longer even to keep up the farce which has been playing for the last year. It will no longer answer the purpose of deceiving the public.

The masonic institution and its votaries are in high favor with the dominant party, who eagerly embrace the most vindictive opponents of General Jackson, if they only come recommended by a strong adhesion

Address of the Minority of the Members of the New York Legislature of 1831, quoted by George E. Baker, ed., *The Works of William H. Seward* (New York: Redfield Co., 1853), III, 347–49.

to the mystic fraternity, or by a violent hatred to anti-masonry. For ourselves, we rejoice at this state of things; we rejoice that the adhering members of this dangerous institution are brought together in one solid mass, that they are arranged in direct and distinct opposition to free inquiry, and to individual and political independence. We rejoice that the question of masonry and anti-masonry is thus presented fairly and openly to the people, stripped of all former political names and associations.

If virtue yet abide among us, if there be intelligence in our fellow-citizens to appreciate the dangers which threaten their liberty, and if there be patriotism to resist and prevent them, which we most firmly believe, there can be no doubt of the result of such a contest. On the one side is an aristocratic nobility, composed of men bound together by the most terrific oaths, which conflict with the administration of justice, with private rights, and with the public security; a privileged order, claiming and securing to its members unequal advantages over their fellow-citizens, veiling its proceedings from scrutiny by pledges of secrecy, collecting funds to unknown amounts and for unknown purposes, and operating through our extended country at any time and on any subject, with all the efficacy of perfect organization, controlled and directed by unseen and unknown hands. On the other side, a portion of your fellow-citizens ask for equal rights and equal privileges among the freemen of this country. They say it is in vain that this equality of rights and privileges is secured in theory by our constitutions and laws, if, by a combination to subvert it, it is in fact no longer enjoyed. They point you to masonic oaths, and to the effects of those dreadful obligations upon our elections, upon witnesses in courts of justice, and upon jurors. They show you one of your citizens murdered under their influence, and the offenders escaping with impunity. They exhibit to you the power of your courts defied, and the administration of justice defeated, through the instrumentality of those obligations. And they ask you whether our country can any longer be described as a land "where no man is so powerful as to be above the law, and no one so humble as to be beneath its protection." They say to you that no man can tell who will be the next victim of masonic vengeance, or of masonic perjury. And they will call on you to put an end to these enormities, and prevent their recurrence, by destroying their source; and for that purpose to use the only effective weapon in your power; a weapon yet preserved to you, your own free and independent ballots. For thus calling on you, they are reproached with being intolerant and proscriptive. For seeking to destroy an institution which will not tolerate any inquiry into its objects, its means, or its obligations, we are intolerant; and for refusing to vote for men who have practically proscribed all who do not belong to their fraternity, we are called proscriptive. For insisting on the enjoyment of equal rights and equal privileges with them, we are charged with denying to our fellow-citizens equal rights.

The Crusade Abandoned

The Antimasons, as a political party, had as their primary opponents the Jacksonians. But if the crusade was to be aimed at Masonry, then Jacksonians and Masons had to be portrayed as one in
the same. This the Antimasons did, and once having proclaimed the
connection, the Antimasons had to contest Jacksonian policies and
power on not just the one issue of Masonry but on all issues. Such
a broadening of the Antimasons' program was inevitable once they
were committed to the attempt to attain political power. That decision having been made, Antimasonry was bound to be submerged
in the discussion of many other issues, local and national, of the
time.

Resolved, That the present administration of this state, has proved
itself entirely incompetent to all the following great and leading objects
of government: The preservation of the funds and property of the state;
the enforcing the demands of public justice; the securing the rights of
citizens by equal legislation; the improving the moral condition of the
people by necessary alteration in our jurisprudence; and the elevating
the character, increasing the wealth, and developing the resources of the
state, by means of internal improvement.

Resolved, That the attempt, by the present administration, known
as the Albany regency, to relieve the banks from the just proportion of
the burthen of government, by imposing a tax upon the people, shows
palpably their imbecility and gross injustice.

Resolved, That the attempt of the administration, to levy a direct

From Proceedings of the Anti-Masonic Convention for the State of New
York held at Utica, August 11, 1830. This tract is to be found in the
Benno Loewy Collection of the Cornell University Library.

tax of more than three hundred thousand dollars, upon the people, to fill a treasury exhausted by its own improvidence and prodigality, justly calls forth the reprobation of the people.

Resolved, That the prosperity of the state of New York is identified with the policy of the protecting system, and works of internal improvement. That the present administration has deceived the people in relation to the former, while it has pursued the cruel policy of a stepmother towards the latter: That the Albany regency, in relation to the canals, have shown themselves incapable of appreciating their value, or pursuing the policy which will preserve them.

Resolved, That in accordance with the principles in the foregoing resolutions expressed, this convention recommend to the electors of this state, as candidate for the office of governor, FRANCIS GRANGER, of the county of Ontario, in whom the people will recognize a man of distinguished talents, pure republicanism, and the fearless advocate of all the rights and interests of the whole people.

FROM THE CONVENTION PRESIDENT'S ADDRESS

A subject heretofore much agitated will require from us little discussion, because it is exclusively within the action of the federal government, and public opinion seems to have finally determined its course, and immovably settled its policy. The protecting system for the industry of the country, is essentially the result of southern policy and southern efforts. The embargo gave the first powerful impulse to manufacturing employments. The non-intercourse and war increased the establishments devoted to that branch of national industry, in strength and numbers. The tariff of 1816, advocated by southern statesmen and carried by southern votes, extended the protection and the justice of the government to those great and growing interests which had been created and fostered by governmental acts. The eastern states, more essentially commercial, opposed the system and reluctantly submitted to its adoption. New and increasing wants of the manufacturing establishments, produced by the changing condition of the world, required for them further protection, and it has been afforded. Relying upon the faith and policy of the nation, vast amounts of capital have been diverted from other employments and invested in those new interests which the acts of the government forced into existence. In those interests great numbers of our fellow citizens are now employed, and every other great interest of the country, has profited by enlarging the field of labor, and multiplying its rewards.

In vain will southern statesmen of southern feelings, or *northern* men with *southern* sympathies, demand of us, for their gratification, the relinquishment of the boon which their policy conferred. The abandonment of the American system, would now produce extended desolation and ruin. Its continuance is now most essential to the agricultural interest. Without it, the surplus products of the soil would find no adequate market, and industry no sufficient reward. In addition to sustaining the price of other agricultural products, its continuance multiplies the subjects of employment and wealth, and will soon constitute the wool of the north, formerly an almost unmerchantable commodity, as safe a dependence and as rich a source of income; as the cotton of the south.

> Issues other than Masonry were presented at the Utica Convention in 1830 and these became more prominent in the next two years. In the quotations from the *Anti-Masonic Enquirer* we see these other issues discussed and should note how, though the attempt was made to keep Antimasonry in the discussion, it became more an afterthought than a central issue.

After a lengthy discussion and denunciation of a tax on goods shipped on the Erie Canal, the editor noted:

> Perhaps the knowledge that this tax would press most heavily upon the farmers of the "infected district" entered into the motives which prompted its imposition. They must be punished for their rebellion to these royal arch rulers [the New York State Democratic Administration]. And what punishment so fit as to make vassals to the powers that be, and compel them to buy the privilege of cultivating their own farms at a king's ransom.

In June 1830, the paper denounced Jackson's Indian policy, and the following year the Bank issue drew most of the editor's commentary. The tariff, the nullification question, and Jackson's land policy were

From the *Anti-Masonic Enquirer*, March 30, 1830.

discussed at length. In all cases the *Enquirer*'s editor was anti-Jackson. By the Antimasons' logic—that Jackson and the Masons were identical —this meant that the paper was still Antimason, but the connection was tenuous and increasingly the editor neglected it. Just before election day in 1832, the *Enquirer*'s editor warned:

> The supremacy of the laws, the safety of the Constitution, the integrity of the Union, the independence of the judicial and legislative departments, the speedy abolition of Freemasonry all depend on the result.

But these warnings were based on such things as Jackson's use of the veto, his challenge of the Supreme Court in the Cherokee case, his party's supposed support of nullification—they were not based simply on the fact that Jackson was a Mason.

Was the Crusade Used Dishonestly by Its Political Leaders?

Jabbez Hammond

Whenever a crusade becomes the basis for political action, questions arise as to whether it is a device employed by self-interested politicians and persons. As suggested in the preceding essay, crusaders are bound to be moved by a combination of selfish and selfless motives. In his history of New York State politics, written in 1846, Jabbez Hammond, a participant in that political life, asked a friend who had been an Antimason to summarize the history of the party. Though certainly not to be accepted as definitive, this writer's assessment of the party makes clear at least one man's conviction that Antimasons were honestly concerned about the Fraternity and, more importantly, it notes that the crusading spirit was so intense that politicians not honestly committed to the crusade's cause could not have used it. Perhaps most important is the author's claim that rather than serving as a valuable weapon to use against Jackson men in New York, the commitment to the Antimasonic crusade proved to be a political liability and strengthened the Jacksonians position in the State.

. . . At many of their town meetings in the spring of 1827, they resolved and acted upon the resolution, that no adhering free mason was worthy to receive the votes of freemen for any office; and by their votes, they excluded free masons from office. It is impossible now to say, which town first set his example, of bringing the subject of free masonry to the test of the ballot box; the movements in this respect were nearly simultaneous in several towns in Genesee and Monroe counties. It is impossible too, to say, whether these movements were

From Jabbez D. Hammond, *The History of Political Parties in the State of New York* (4th ed., Cooperstown, N.Y., 1846), I, 378–97. Hammond tells his readers that this section was written for him by an Antimason.

first commenced by the opponents of free masonry, to put down the institution, or by the free masons to put down the committees. Each, probably, commenced the movement in different towns. The feeling rose so strong and fierce on both sides that it was evident that it must find vent somewhere; and it was fortunate for the country that the nature of our institutions furnished a constitutional vent, where so little harm would be done. Thus, in fact, political anti-masonry had its commencement. It presented but a single point, the destruction of free masonry through the instrumentality of the ballot boxes. People at first arrayed themselves on each side of this question—with reference to this question alone—and with utter disregard of all previous political designations and distinctions. It was emphatically a spontaneous movement of the people themselves, not only in absence of, but in defiance of the counsels of political leaders. It was, in truth and reality, a spontaneous outbreak of popular impulse, prompted by no leader, guided by no politician. Its first and principal purpose was to aid in the execution of the laws by the ballot box; to strengthen the arm of justice by the elective franchise.

It is not necessary here, nor does it come within the scope of this treatise at all, to say whether the views of the anti-masons were right or wrong; whether their principle of exclusion of free masons was worthy or unworthy of themselves or the country; whether their manner of political action was justifiable or prudent or otherwise: those topics may find an appropriate place in a treatise of another character. In order to show fairly the causes of the rise of the anti-masonic party, as a political party, it has been deemed necessary to say thus much of its origin, as its rise is intimately connected with the outrage upon Morgan; but the history of that transaction, important though it may be in another point of view, will only be adverted to here as connected with the rise and progress of the political party whose history is now under consideration.

Though this was the starting point of anti-masonry as a political party, yet it is not to be understood that this party even then, or until some considerable time afterwards, assumed the perfect form and feature of an organized party. The town elections above mentioned were the results of the desultory and spontaneous efforts of the people themselves in different towns. Those who were generally considered as political leaders were mostly averse to taking political ground in this manner. Their old party ties and associations were still cherished; and practised politicians upon either side were averse to abandoning the parties with which they had so long acted. Some of them desired to preserve and continue the old party organization, but so to conduct their respective operations as to prevent the nomination of masons by the conventions of either political party. In this way it was hoped by some, that masonry could be effectually put down in a quiet manner, without incurring the imputation of removing old political landmarks, or dissolving old political associations. If reflection did not, subsequent circumstances did show, that all such speculations were idle. Masons were no more willing to be proscribed in the conventions than at the polls, and it might have been foreseen that one party or the other would bid for their aid. The then posture of political parties, both in regard to state and national politics, may, and probably did, have something to do in making anti-masonry political. Mr. Clinton had been elected governor, and it began by this time to be understood that he would unite with Mr. Van Buren in the support of Gen. Jackson for the presidency. This determination of Mr. Clinton was not acceptable to many of his political friends. On the other hand, a large portion of the bucktails at the west were dissatisfied with the former movement of their political friends to force the nomination of Mr. Crawford; they were suspicious that the recent election of Mr. Clinton was produced by the supineness if not treachery of their political friends at the east, and they were jealous of the reputed union between Mr. Clinton and Mr. Van Buren to secure the vote of the state for Gen. Jackson. All these circumstances gave the politicians of the Clintonian party, opposed to Gen. Jackson, who were upon the committees of investigation, a convenient opportunity, by operating upon the prevalent public sentiment against masonry, to direct the attention of those who were thus hostile to masonry, to the fact that both Gov. Clinton and General Jackson were high masons, and that their political union was another evidence of masonic influence, and thus stimulate this sentiment to the opposition of both. The Clintonian committee men could, in this mode, present the appearance of magnanimity in giving up their own cherished leader, and with the better grace ask the bucktails in like manner to give up Gen. Jackson, whom, without the interference of anti-masonry, that party would have very generally supported. As the situation of political parties at that time furnished shrewd and calculating politicians with opportunities for so directing the prevalent public feeling, it has been supposed that they took advantage of it to give such direction to public action. Possibly something of this kind may have been done or attempted; yet a careful consideration of the state of public sentiment at that time must satisfy any one that but little could have been effected in this way. In a state of high excitement in any community few can remain cool and unaffected by the prevalent public sentiment; and those that do, by not entering into the feeling themselves, have seldom the power of giving direction to public feeling. Those who are excited themselves will receive directions and suggestions only from those who are heartily and earnestly imbued with the same general feeling.

The truth is, the public were highly excited, and the excitement pervaded all classes of people. If the more practised politicians were desirous of giving a different direction to the public feeling, they found it was substantially out of their power. The people had themselves determined to bring the subject of free masonry to the test of the ballot box, laying out of view all other political questions, and those who felt with them were constrained to follow the popular impulse. The investigation of the abduction during the summer of 1827 had made many converts to this sentiment, and before the fall elections came on, those who were determined to make masonry a test at the elections, were a majority in several counties, though the fact was not generally believed until after the elections were held. During all this time, and indeed during the whole contest, the masons complained of this course as unjust and proscriptive. And on the other hand the anti-masons, even while preparing their tickets for the canvass, strenuously insisted that their objects were not political. They seemed at first to have had an earnest desire to escape the imputation of making anti-masonry a political party. Their probable object in doing this, while they avowed they would not vote for a mason for office, was to inform the existing political parties, that as to the political grounds upon which they were divided, they should neither commit themselves or take sides. They only committed themselves not to support a mason of any party; and as neither political party would adopt that rule of exclusion, they were forced to run a ticket of their own; but by so doing, they did not mean to consider themselves bound to support the measures of either political party. They had an object of their own to accomplish, which was of paramount importance in their estimation, and they asked all citizens of whatever former politics, to aid them in the accomplishment of this object. By this general invitation they would offend the previous political feelings or prejudices of none. If this invitation was accepted by the mass of the voters, the former political parties would be broken up and destroyed. This result was of course foreseen by the politicians of all parties. The political leaders were, however, desirous of preserving the organization of the respective parties. Many of them were not sufficiently imbued with the spirit of hostility to the masons to take ground with the new party; many of them thought the basis of the anti-masonic party was too narrow and proscriptive to meet with success; or, if it was successful, that the ascendancy would be temporary and ephemeral; and so they determined to stand by their old party discipline and usages. This was rather the feeling previous to the election of 1827. The bucktails made their nominations—the Adams party made theirs—and the anti-masons made theirs without any regard to previous political distinctions. The result astonished all—even the anti-masons themselves—and opened the eyes of politicians to the growing power of this new party. At this election, the anti-masons carried Genesee, Monroe, Livingston, Orleans and Niagara counties, in face of both the other parties.

At this election, the candidates of the Adams party received but few votes comparatively. The candidates of the bucktail party took by far the largest share of the votes which were not cast for anti-masonry, in the counties where anti-masonry was made a question. The final result of the operation of anti-masonry upon the existing political parties was faintly foreshadowed by its evident effect in this election in these few counties. A large majority of the masons, in both political parties, felt themselves proscribed by the rule which the anti-masons had adopted, and would, from this feeling, vote with the party which showed the greatest strength, antagonistical, to anti-masonry. Many of the prominent members of both parties also, who were not masons, and who were willing to see the outrage investigated, were yet unwilling to give up their party organization, and, perhaps, thought that it was unjust and impolitic to preclude every member of the masonic fraternity from holding office. Some of the politicians of the old Clintonian party were, by their associations, thrown into the Jackson party, so that parties in the west essentially changed ground. The incipient Jackson party was formed of a portion of the old and regular bucktail party—a majority of the masons who felt themselves aggrieved by the application of the anti-masonic principle—and some of the leading Clintonians. The Adams party was left with but few in numbers: composed mostly of Clintonians, who, though masons, were unwilling to join the Jackson party and could not act with the anti-masons, and some Clintonians who were not masons, and were unwilling to act with either of the other parties. The anti-masonic party was composed of a large majority of the old Clintonian party, and indeed almost the entire party, with the above exceptions, and a very considerable portion of the bucktail party, comprising a great force in votes at the polls, and, perhaps, not a great force of the old political leaders. It is to be observed, that these remarks are to be deemed to be confined to the western counties, commonly called "the infected district," where anti-masonry had its origin.

A new party thus organized, like the anti-masonic party, of materials never before accustomed to be assimilated, comparatively without leaders, and having but one object in view, and moved by a feeling of high excitement, would not be likely to be choice in the selection of their candidates. There is a strong instance of this in the election of 1827. An anti-masonic convention for the 8th senatorial district was held in that year for the nomination of an anti-masonic candidate for senator. They were somewhat at a loss who to take in the immaturity of the party, and selected with imprudent haste and without due inquiry, George A. S. Crooker, as their candidate, and he was formally announced as such, and votes regularly printed and distributed for him. The anti-masonic committee at Rochester ascertained that Mr. Crooker was not only a mason, but that he was in other respects an unworthy candidate for any party, and recommended that Timothy H. Porter, the nominee of the bucktail party, should receive the suffrages of the anti-masons. This recommendation, though given upon the eve of the election, was effective; Crooker was dropped and Mr. Porter was elected by a large majority.

During this time there were many secessions from the masonic fraternity, and the seceding members not only confirmed the truth of Morgan's "Illustrations" of the first degrees of masonry, but penetrated farther into the arcana of the masonic mysteries, and disclosed the ceremonies and obligations of several of the higher degrees of masonry. These disclosures induced the anti-masons to receive the seceding members into their fellowship, and welcome them with warmth into their ranks, with every assurance of protection. They contributed also to still further excite the public feeling in the western counties against the institution, and to prompt them to greater exertions to abolish it through the medium of the ballot-box. The institution was now looked upon as based on principles dangerous in a free government, subversive of political equality, and hostile to the impartial administration of justice. The overthrow of the institution was now the principal object to be accomplished, and the abduction of Morgan was referred to as one among the many evidences of the dangerous and secret power of free masonry. Converts to the side of anti-masonry increased rapidly. In March, 1828, the first general convention was held at Le Roy upon this subject, and was composed of delegates from twelve of the western counties. The delegates were numerous and highly respectable for their standing and character. The whole scope of the proceedings of this convention was to present to the public the dangerous principles of free masonry, to excite attention to it, and evoke action against it. This, as at the first, was the only point to which action was asked. There was no political resolution passed, except that which declared that free masonry was unworthy to exist in a free government. Yet this convention was political in its object in this sense, that it endeavored to bring public opinion to bear upon the institution of free masonry through the ballot box; and the better to effect that object, they recommended the calling of a state convention at Utica, in August following. At the Le Roy convention, Samuel Works, Henry Ely, Frederick F. Bachus, Frederick Whittlesey and Thurlow Weed were appointed a general central committee. These gentlemen were continued in that station by subsequent state conventions, and with the addition of Bates Cook and Timothy Fitch, held it as long as anti-masonry continued to be a separate and distinct party.

The object of calling the convention at Utica, in August, was not stated to be for the purpose of nominating anti-masonic candidates for governor and lieutenant governor; but it was very generally understood that such step would be taken by that convention; and it was almost equally generally believed, that Francis Granger would be the nominee of the anti-masons for the office of governor.

The other political parties were actively engaged in the presidential contest, to be decided at the ensuing election, and watching with keen interest the course of events which might affect their several political prospects. The national republican party supported Mr. Adams as their candidate for president. It was apparent that this party could have no hope of success for their state ticket, unless they could secure to its aid the anti-masonic vote. As a majority of the anti-masons were from this party, it did not seem to its leaders difficult to command their support. They supposed that by calling their state convention first, and so far yielding to the anti-masonic sentiment as to put in nomination candidates who were not masons, particularly if Mr. Granger, the expected candidate of the anti-masons, was put upon the ticket, the anti-masons, at their convention would cordially respond to such nominations and their success secured. The national republicans did call their state convention, which was held a few days in advance of the time selected for the meeting of the anti-masonic convention, and nominated Judge Smith Thompson as their candidate for governor, and Francis Granger as their candidate for lieutenant governor. The anti-masons were almost universally dissatisfied with this movement of the national republicans, and thought that they had resorted to this expedient to prostrate the anti-masonic nominations and stifle anti-masonry in the embrace of a mere political party. Anti-masonry had taken the ground that it could carry the question of masonry to the polls, and believing this to be a matter of greater importance and higher moment than any mere political question, and being eager and enthusiastic in the cause, they determined in any event to make nominations distinctly on that ground, and compel the national republican party to accept them or lose the state. In other words the anti-masons wished to force the national republicans to wield their political strength to aid in the destruction of the masonic institution, and consequently, though Judge Thompson was no mason, and Mr. Granger was a favorite with the anti-masons, the national republican nominations not being placed upon anti-masonic grounds, met with no favor from the anti-masons. Indeed if the national republican convention had nominated precisely the same individuals whom the anti-masons would have themselves nominated, yet it is probable that the anti-masons would not have responded even to such nominations.

Soon after these nominations were made, the anti-masonic convention met at Utica. The following resolution, adopted as a measure necessary "to counteract the influence and destroy the existence of masonic societies," records the position in which the anti-masonic party then desired to place themselves before the public:

"6. That it is expedient for this convention, in pursuit of the good objects to be accomplished, wholly to disregard the two great political parties that at this time distract this state and the union, in the choice of candidates for office; and to nominate anti-masonic candidates for governor and lieutenant governor."

The anti-masonic convention did nominate such candidates. Mr. Granger not having, at that time, accepted the previous nomination, he was now nominated as candidate for governor, and John Crary of Washington county, as candidate for lieutenant governor. These two gentlemen had recommended themselves to the favor of the anti-masonic party by their course in the legislature, the former in the assembly, and the latter in the senate, upon questions connected with the abduction of Morgan, which were presented for legislative action. After the adjournment of this convention, Mr. Granger had two invitations before him to stand as the candidate of the respective conventions, but for different offices. He could not well accept both, and there was great interest felt, to know how he would decide. His political sentiments were known to be in favor of Mr. Adams and his measures; and he also approved to a great extent of the anti-masonic action. He was, in fact, what might then be called a national republican anti-mason; designations which just at that time came into collision, and were in some sense inconsistent with each other. He doubtless wished, in common with many others, to see the whole available opposition to General Jackson brought to act in concert and harmony. Whether he supposed it was possible to effect this object is doubtful; but he had been committed by his friends in some degree to both sides. His was then a difficult and delicate position, and he suffered some time to elapse, probably with the hope of removing all the difficulties before he made his decision. If he had any such hope, he found it a vain one, and finally decided by declining the anti-masonic nomination for the higher office, and accepting that for the secondary office, which had been tendered him first. He foresaw that neither ticket could be successful, as harmony and concert were impracticable; and he thought, probably, that it was both more candid, honorable and politic to accept the nomination first tendered. This decision excited the hopes of the national republicans, and the anger of the anti-masons. With the latter, Mr. Granger passed at once from the station of a popular favorite, to become the object of bitter denunciation. The anti-masons were resolved not to be foiled in their determination to have a candidate of their own, either by the movements of the national republicans, or the declination of their own nominee. They were disappointed by this declination; but the disappointment produced heat, excitement and prompt action, instead of inaction or despondency. But their zeal and energy, in this emergency, far exceeded their discretion and good judgment in the selection of the person to supply Mr. Granger's place.

Solomon Southwick of Albany, had previously played a conspicuous part in the political history of this state. He was, at all times, vain and egotistical in his claims to personal consequence, visionary and unsound in his political views, and unstable and wavering in his political course. These defects of character and the conduct naturally flowing from them, had at the time anti-masonry broke out, reduced him to poverty in pecuniary resources, and discredit in political reputation. He conducted a newspaper in Albany. He had been a mason. He acquired some credit with the anti-masons by an early renunciation of his masonic ties and denunciation of the masonic institution. His own movements plainly showed that he wished to turn the circumstance to account, both to add to the support of his paper and advance his own visionary projects of personal ambition. He acted in concert with many masons at the west in preparing a general renunciation and exposition of free masonry. General meetings for this object were held at Le Roy, in January and July, 1828, at which Mr. Southwick was a conspicuous member. On occasion of one of his visits to the west, he was invited by a few seceding masons to stand as candidate for governor. A correspondence was duly had and published; Mr. Southwick expressing a willingness to be used as a candidate. The general sentiment of the anti-masons did not respond to this movement, and it was looked upon as an abortion. The declination of Mr. Granger, and the angry feeling with which it was received by the anti-masons generally, furnished a good opportunity for these ardent friends of

Mr. Southwick to renew their movement. A few of them met at Le Roy and put him in nomination for the place vacated by Mr. Granger. The anti-masonic committees made no concerted movement to have a new candidate regularly brought out; the mass were angry at Mr. Granger: determined to have some candidate of their own, they did not care who, and they gradually and of their own accord, fell in with the nomination of Mr. Southwick.

It may be safely assumed that politicians of the Jackson or Tammany party did what they could to favor this movement and fan the excitement, that by the division of the other party, they might secure the election of Mr. Van Buren. But such extraneous influences were to a great degree unnecessary; the excited feelings of the anti-masons did what no mere calculating policy could effect. It was in vain that the better informed and more sagacious of the anti-masons warned them that the character of Mr. Southwick was such as would discredit any party at whose head he might be placed. It was in vain that several of the county conventions refused to concur in the nomination. The people were excited and determined to have a candidate. They thought they had been maneuvered out of one, and they resented it; and it was no matter what the character or fitness of Mr. Southwick was, they knew they could not elect him, but they would show by their votes for him that they had an energy and spirit which could not be deceived or subdued. And Mr. Southwick was in fact adopted by the mass of the people in the western counties as their candidate.

The election came. Mr. Van Buren received one hundred and thirty-six thousand seven hundred and ninety-four votes; Judge Thompson one hundred and six thousand four hundred and forty-four, and Solomon Southwick thirty-three thousand three hundred and forty-five; the latter mostly from the western counties. Mr. Van Buren was thus elected by a minority vote; but such were the jealousies between the national republicans and anti-masons, that it is doubtful whether any practical plan could have been devised by which the entire opposition vote could have been united upon one man and thus defeated Mr. Van Buren. It is certain that if anti-masonry had had no existence, Mr. Van Buren must have been elected, as anti-masonry in the western counties drew off a large detachment of voters from the support of Jackson and Van Buren; and many of the former friends of Mr. Clinton would have contributed, as they did, to increase the Jackson and Van Buren vote.

As General Jackson was a high mason, and Mr. Adams was not a mason, the anti-masons united with the national republicans, in the support of Adams electors; and the electoral vote of the state was, in consequence, nearly equally divided. The Jackson party, of course, carried a majority in the state legislature; but the anti-masons and national republicans elected a respectable number of members. As yet, neither of the great political parties in the state seemed willing to come to an open quarrel with the anti-masons: indeed, they both showed some evidence of a desire to caress, conciliate and use it for their purposes. Anti-masonry all this time aimed to stand independent of and in opposition to both.

Gov. Van Buren, in his message to the legislature in January, 1829, referred to the subject of the excitement growing out of the abduction of Morgan in terms of moderate commendation, and deprecated the perversion of this feeling to selfish and sinister purposes. It was evidently intended to convey the idea that the excitement created by a great and local cause was worthy of the people among whom it found existence; but its direction to political objects was unworthy their good sense and intelligence.

Although the anti-masons claimed to stand independent of both political parties; and although, as a party, they had neither avowed nor expressed any opinion upon the great and leading measures of the country, yet it soon became evident that this party must eventually be forced into opposition to the Jackson party. Gen. Jackson himself was a high mason, and could not, upon the fundamental principles of anti-masonry, in any event, be supported by them. The anti-masons required a civil proscription of masons. The Jackson party in the state could not yield to this requirement without breaking up the bonds of their strength and perilling its power; and the anti-masonic members of the state legislature generally went with the national republicans as to measures. All these circumstances clearly indicated that the anti-masonic party must eventually be forced into opposition to the Jackson party. Doubtless, Gov. Van Buren perceived this when he penned his message to the legislature in 1829.

The anti-masonic party held a convention at Albany in February, 1829. Its object was to strengthen themselves, extend their influence, spread information, and advise all that they were neither discouraged nor disheartened. Its proceedings were similar to those of former conventions, and directed exclusively against free masonry.

The national republican party, though they polled so large a vote in 1828, soon found that they had not strength to effect much of themselves, and as an independent and separate party, they dwindled into inertness and inactivity. They were not ready to unite cordially with the anti-masons, and they had no separate power of their own to use with effect. The anti-masons were enthusiastic, persevering and energetic. At the election in 1829, they elected Albert H. Tracy senator from the eighth district by a majority of about eight thousand votes, and carried the counties of Erie, Niagara, Orleans, Genesee, Livingston, Monroe, Allegany, Cattaraugus, Chautauqua, Steuben, Ontario, Wayne, Yates, Seneca and Washington, and polled, as is computed, about sixty-seven thousand votes.

At the session of the legislature of 1830, Lieut. Gov. Throop, then acting governor, in his message, alluded to the anti-masonic excitement with less of dignity and more of petulance than had characterized the preceding message. He speaks of it as originating "in an honest zeal overflowing its proper boundaries, misdirected in its efforts and carrying into public affairs, matters properly belonging to social discipline." He further intimates that these feelings "give evidence of speedily subsiding into their natural and healthful channel." It seems quite apparent from the tone of this message, and the legislative and executive action during the ensuing session, that the Jackson party now found that they must stand in full opposition to the anti-masonic party, and they probably indulged in some apprehensions as to the power of a party who had nearly doubled their vote in a single year, and who were bold, confident and resolute in their action. At any rate legislative action at this session was more than commonly hostile to the views of the anti-masons, who went on with their investigations of the Morgan outrage, their persecution of free masonry, and their political movements *pari passu,* and made each bear upon the other.

The anti-masons again held a convention at Albany in February, 1830. After providing for calling a national convention to be held at Philadelphia, and a state convention for the nomination of governor, they prepared specific charges against the grand chapter of the state, for furnishing funds to aid the Morgan conspirators in escaping from justice, and thus interfering to defeat the due administration of the laws. A memorial on that subject was drawn up and presented to the legislature then in session, praying for the appointment of a committee of that body to investigate the conduct of the grand chapter in this respect, inasmuch as said chapter had received an act of incorporation from the legislature. The legislature, by a vote of seventy-five to thirty, in effect refused the committee, by referring the whole subject to the attorney general, and if he should find the grand chapter guilty, to file a *quo warranto.* This was not what the anti-masons wanted, nor was it of any use to them in their inquiries concerning the grand chapter, inasmuch as proof of the charges must be made before a *quo warranto* would be granted, and this proof could be obtained only from members of the chapter, who would not volunteer it; and the sole object the anti-masons had in asking for a legislative committee, was by this means to force proof from the members of the chapter. The anti-masons deemed that by this vote, the majority of the legislature had declared themselves hostile to inquiry into the misdeeds of masonry. Another circumstance operated very strongly upon the anti-masons to induce a settled conviction in their minds that the political majority were hostile to them in every way, even in the prosecution of the investigation. In the winter of 1828, a law for the appointment of special counsel to investigate the Morgan outrage, unasked for and even opposed by the anti-masons, was, upon the recommendation of acting Governor Pitcher, passed. Judge Mosely was first appointed to that office. After his resignation, Mr. John C. Spencer received the appointment. He prosecuted the duties of this office with his usual indefatigable industry and effective ability. He had traced the web of the criminal mystery with such considerable success, that he thought by the application of the reward of two thousand dollars which Gov. Clinton had previously offered, he should be able to solve the whole mystery of Morgan's murder. He wrote to Gov. Throop for advice and authority to so use the money. The authority was refused. Mr. Spencer's report to the legislature bore very hard upon the western masons. It was of a tone calculated to aid the anti-masons politically. There was considerable prospect that the whole conspiracy would finally be developed. This would strengthen the anti-masons. The legislature, so far from giving any hearty approval of Mr. Spencer's very efficient proceedings, cut down his salary to one thousand dollars. Mr. Spencer and the whole body of the anti-masons deemed this a studied and intentional insult. Mr. Spencer resigned, and in his letter of resignation complained that he had received no effective aid or assistance from the executive, and that even his confidential communications to the governor in relation to the conspiracy had been disclosed to the counsel for the conspirators. From all this, the anti-masons felt themselves authorized to charge, and did charge the dominant party with the protection of masonry, and the conspirators in the Morgan outrage. From this time the anti-masonic party stood in decided hostility to the Jackson party, and now openly avowed what they had before in fact, been acting upon, opposition to the dominant party.

All these movements prepared the anti-masonic party to look solely to the extension of their own peculiar principles, and to the aid of the national republicans for success. A convention was held at Utica in August, 1830. Here, for the *first time*, in an anti-masonic convention, were opinions avowed upon important political measures. These opinions, now avowed, were in general accordance with those opposed to the dominant party; and were, doubtless, made public with a view to obtain the support of those who, though disagreeing with them upon the subject of free masonry, still otherwise held to the same common political principles. The anti-masons very soon forgot their brief indignation against Mr. Granger for declining their first nomination. He had subsequently acted with them, and manifested so much constancy and ability, that he was entirely restored to their affections and confidence. Mr. Granger was nominated as candidate for governor, and Samuel Stevens of New-York, as candidate for lieutenant governor. Gov. Throop was the opposing candidate. The national republicans generally concurred in the nomination of Messrs. Granger and Stevens; and the prospect seemed fair for their election. Gov. Throop was far from being the strongest man in his own party, and was certainly not strong at the west. Mr. Granger commanded the enthusiastic support of the anti-masons, and the cordial aid of the national republicans. He was not considered personally proscriptive, whatever might be thought of the principles of anti-masonry generally; and he was, on the whole, the strongest man on that side that could be selected. If the national republicans, who adhered to free masonry in the eastern and central counties, had merged their strong and unmitigated hatred to anti-masonry, in their attachment to their professed political principles, which these hated anti-masons supported, and like a majority of their own party, cast their votes for the candidates nominated by the anti-masons, the whole political complexion of the state would probably have been changed at this election. But persons of this class felt persecuted and oppressed by political anti-masonry, and voted against its candidates; not because they liked Jacksonism better, but because they hated anti-masonry more. The election came and was warmly contested. Mr. Throop received one hundred twenty-eight thousand eight hundred and forty-two votes, and Mr. Granger one hundred and twenty thousand three hundred and sixty-one. Mr. Throop's majority being a little more than eight thousand. This election had the effect to throw permanently into the Jackson party, numbers who, if anti-masonry had not been a question, would have been national republicans.

Suggested Readings

The propensity of Americans in the 1820's and the 1830's to engage in crusades is noted in Marvin Meyer, *The Jacksonian Persuasion* (Stanford, Calif.: Stanford University Press, 1957); Lee Benson, *The Concept of Jacksonian Democracy* (Princeton, N.J.: Princeton University Press, 1961); and Whitney Cross, *The Burned Over District* (New York: Harper Torchbooks, 1965). Cross' work has been justly influential, but perhaps because it was a pioneering effort—and a good one—it has been accepted too uncritically. The conditions Cross cites as explanation for what motivated men to join crusades are too specific, as we have noted in the introductory essay to this volume. The presence of crusades in America needs much more examination than it has received. Richard Hofstadter's essay, "The Paranoid Style in American Politics," in his book of essays of the same name (New York: Vintage, 1964); and the David B. Davis article, "Some Themes of Counter-Subversion . . . ," *Mississippi Valley Historical Review,* XLVII (September, 1960), 205–24 are good starting points.

The history of the Masons has been left primarily to Masons to write and so is neither objective nor analytical. Bernard Fay, *Revolution and Freemasonry 1680–1800* (Boston: Little, Brown, 1935) is the most useful work, but Fay's claims as to the influence of the Fraternity in causing both the American and the French Revolutions seem much exaggerated, and in any case, they are not substantiated. Vernon Stauffer, *New England and the Bavarian Illuminati* (New York: Columbia University Press, 1918) is the best study of that Antimasonic outburst of the late eighteenth century. It is interesting, and it is unfortunate, that those who have studied the politics of that era have neglected the Masonic controversy. Even James Smith, *Freedom's Fetters* (Ithaca, N.Y.: Cornell University Press, 1956); and Leonard Levy, *Freedom of Speech and Press in Early American History* (New York: Harper Torchbooks, 1963) in their studies of the threat to

liberty have neglected the subject. Though not a major incident, the presence of Antimasonry sentiment in that era provides sufficient evidence of
the fear of conspiracy and the concern about national security so that the
implications deserve attention.

The only general account of Antimasonry in the 1820's and the 1830's
is Charles McCarthy, "The Antimasonic Party," *American Historical Association Annual Report for the Year 1902*, I (Washington, 1903), 369–
574. McCarthy is obviously influenced by the Turnerian explanation of
the rise of democracy on the frontier and the conflict of frontier democrats
with Eastern urban elements. Though not accepting the frontier part of
the theory, Lee Benson has accepted McCarthy's conclusion that Anti-
masonry, at least in New York, was an egalitarian movement. I am not
prepared to say that Benson is wrong, but the Antimasons' democratic
rhetoric may have been a generally accepted rhetoric and not evidence
that pro and antidemocratic forces were fighting it out. As I have noted,
Antimasons were moralists, and their names crop up in all sorts of moral
crusades. But whether those who sought a moral society were also seekers
after a further democratization of society seems questionable.

Antimasonry, in its political form, is described in David Ludlum,
Social Ferment in Vermont, 1791–1850 (New York: Columbia University
Press, 1939); Dixon Ryan Fox, *The Decline of the Aristocracy in the
Politics of New York* (New York: Harper Torchbooks, 1965), orig. pub.
1918); and Richard McCormick, *The Second American Party System*
(Chapel Hill, N.C.: University of North Carolina Press, 1966).

In an unpublished Ph.D. dissertation entitled "The Antimasonic Persuasion, A Study of Public Address in the American Antimasonic Movement, 1826–1838," presented to the Cornell University Speech Department in 1950, Leland Griffin has collected numerous Antimasonic speeches
and tracts, but Griffin is interested in the rhetoric of Antimasonry and
his work is useful to historians primarily as a guide to available primary
materials. The best collection of those materials is the Benno Loewy Collection found in the Cornell University Library. Like most crusaders, the
Antimasons published hundreds of tracts and also founded many newspapers to spread the word about the evils of the Fraternity. The New York
Historical Society has the best collection of those newspapers. But the
mass of material does not help the historian as much as it might because
it is propaganda. The authors all say much the same thing and reading
the material becomes a matter of much work for little return. The sources
reprinted in this volume are, in my opinion, representative and reflective of
the positions and the changes in position of the Antimasons.